Inside Macintosh® X Ref

Addison-Wesley Publishing Company, Inc.
Reading, Massachusetts   Menlo Park, California   New York
Don Mills, Ontario   Wokingham, England   Amsterdam   Bonn
Sydney   Singapore   Tokyo   Madrid   San Juan

 APPLE COMPUTER, INC.

Copyright © 1988 by Apple Computer, Inc.

All rights reserved. No part of this publication may be reproduced, stored in a retrieval system, or transmitted, in any form or by any means, electronic, mechanical, photocopying, recording, or otherwise, without prior written permission of Apple Computer, Inc. Printed in the United States of America.

Apple, the Apple logo, AppleTalk, A/UX, HyperCard, ImageWriter, MacApp, and Macintosh, are registered trademarks of Apple Computer, Inc.

APDA, Apple Desktop Bus, Finder, and Stackware are trademarks of Apple Computer, Inc.

Helvetica and Times are registered trademarks of Linotype Co.

Microsoft is a registered trademark of Microsoft Corporation.

NuBus is a trademark of Texas Instruments.

POSTSCRIPT is a registered trademark of Adobe Systems Incorporated.

UNIX is a registered trademark of AT&T Information Systems.

Simultaneously published in the United States and Canada.

ISBN 0-201-13694-5
ISBN 0-201-19265-9
CDEFGH-AL-898
Third printing, July 1988

Inside Macintosh X-Ref

Contents

1   **Preface: About This Book**

3   **Index I: General Index**

49   **Index II: Constants and Field Names**

59   **Appendix A: Routines That May Move or Purge Memory**

63   **Appendix B: System Traps**
63   Sorted by Name
72   Sorted by Trap Word

83   **Appendix C: Global Variables**

89   **Glossary**

This book was written, edited, and composed on a desktop publishing system using Apple® Macintosh® computers and Microsoft® Word. Proof and final pages were produced on the Apple LaserWriter® Plus Printer. POSTSCRIPT™, the LaserWriter page-description language, was developed by Adobe Systems Incorporated. The text is set in Times® and the display type in Helvetica®.

PREFACE: ABOUT THIS BOOK

The *Inside Macintosh® X-Ref* is your key to Apple's official programming books for the Macintosh family of computers. The *X-Ref* gives you:

- a general index to eight books: all five volumes of *Inside Macintosh,* the *Programmer's Introduction to the Macintosh Family,* the *Technical Introduction to the Macintosh Family,* and *Designing Cards and Drivers for the Macintosh II and Macintosh SE.* The general index also contains references to the *Macintosh Technical Notes* for 1984–1987.

- a complete list of routines that may move or purge memory

- a list of all Macintosh system traps

- a list of all Macintosh global variables

- a comprehensive Macintosh glossary

In addition, the *Inside Macintosh X-Ref* contains a new index, never before published, listing all constants and field names in *Inside Macintosh.*

The books for which the *Inside Macintosh X-Ref* is a cross-reference are published by Addison-Wesley as part of the Apple Technical Library. *Macintosh Technical Notes* may be ordered from APDA, the Apple Programmer's and Developer's Association. For information about APDA, see the inside back cover of this book.

The text of the *Inside Macintosh X-Ref* is also available from APDA in the form of Macintosh text files on a 3.5-inch disk.

INDEX I: GENERAL INDEX

The General Index lists page references for eight books plus the *Macintosh Technical Notes* for 1984–1987. The eight books include all five volumes of *Inside Macintosh*, the *Programmer's Introduction to the Macintosh Family*, the *Technical Introduction to the Macintosh Family*, and *Designing Cards and Drivers for the Macintosh II and Macintosh SE*.

The index entries for the different books are distinguished by letter codes, as follows:

Code	Book	Sample listing
I, II, III, IV, V	*Inside Macintosh*	II-276 = Volume II, page 276
P	*Programmer's Introduction to the Macintosh Family*	P-103 = page 103
T	*Technical Introduction to the Macintosh Family*	T-78 = page 78
C	*Designing Cards and Drivers for the Macintosh II and Macintosh SE*	C8-12 = chapter 8, page 12
N	*Macintosh Technical Notes*	N2 = Technical Note 2

A

ABByte data type II-276
ABCallType data type II-274
ABPasIntf N132
ABProtoType data type II-274
ABridge low memory global N9
ABRecHandle data type II-274
ABRecPtr data type II-274
ABusRecord data type II-274
 ALAP parameters II-276
 ATP parameters II-287
 DDP parameters II-281
 NBP parameters II-298
ABusVars global variable II-328
AC specifications for line drive (NuBus card) C6-2
access modes V-376
access path II-83, IV-94, T-158
 buffer II-84, IV-96
accesses, non-aligned C3-16
accessing
 files P-130
 menus/menu items P-104
/ACK C2-5, C3-4, C5-6, 7, C6-2
acknowledge cycle C1-8
 defined C2-7

acknowledgement C3-9, C13-8
ACount global variable I-423
'actb' resource V-278
action procedure I-316, 324, 328
 in control definition function I-332
activate event I-244, 279, P-33, T-37, 39, 50
 event message I-252
ActivatePalette procedure V-162
active
 control I-313
 window I-46, 270, 284, T-49
active end IV-5
active-low signal C2-8
ADB device table V-367
ADBDataBlock V-369
ADBOp function V-368
ADBReInit procedure V-367, N143
'ADBS' resource V-371
ADBSetInfoBlock V-370
AddComp procedure V-147
AddDrive function N36, N108
additive primary T-100
AddPt procedure I-193
AddrBlock data type II-281
AddReference N2
AddResMenu procedure I-353, V-243, P-102
AddResource procedure I-124
AddResponse function II-318, V-513

address allocations, Macintosh II C4-5
address/data bus, Macintosh II C1-7
address/data signals C2-5, C3-4
address error T-189
address mapping, NuBus to Macintosh II C4-5
Address Mapping Unit (AMU) C1-6, T-206
address mark II-211
address space T-192, 202, 203
    Macintosh SE C13-16
    Macintosh II C4-2
AddSearch procedure V-147
/AD31–/AD0 C2-5, C3-4, C6-2
A5 register N25
AFP *See* AppleTalk Filing Protocol
AFPCommand function V-542
ALAP *See* AppleTalk Link Access Protocol
ALAP frame II-264
ALAP protocol type II-264
Alarm Clock N85, T-38, 78, 131
alarm clock event T-38
alarm setting T-132
alert I-401, 409, P-105, 109, 167, T-56, 59
    box I-401, T-59
    closing P-107
    color in P-106
    color table V-278
    guidelines I-68
    opening P-107
    posting P-109
    resource format I-426
    stages I-409
    template I-403, 424
    types of P-106
    windows I-401, I-402
Alert function I-418, V-284
AlertTemplate data type I-424
AlertTHndl data type I-425
AlertTPtr data type I-425
alias II-266
aliasing C1-9
A-line instruction T-25
Allocate function IV-143
    high-level II-94
    low-level II-113
allocated block II-10, T-147
allocation block II-79, IV-89
AllocContig function IV-143
    high-level IV-112
    low-level IV-143
AllocCursor procedure V-75
'ALRT' resource V-278
altDBoxProc P-92

American National Standards Institute (ANSI) T-227
amplitude of a wave II-223, T-171
Analog Signal Generator (ASG) T-226
ancestors P-147
anchor point IV-5
AngleFromSlope function I-476
AnimateEntry procedure V-164
AnimatePalette procedure V-164
animating colors V-156
ANS Pascal P-140
ANumber global variable I-423
ApFontID global variable I-219, IV-31
apostrophe T-158
AppendMenu procedure I-352, V-243, P-102
AppFile data type II-58
'APPL' resource N29
Apple DCA filter T-180
Apple Desktop Bus V-361, T-5, 200, 229, 23
    keyboards T-232
    Manager T-22
    mouse T-235
    routines V-367
Apple Developer Services P-157, T-257
Apple Extended Keyboard V-190, 192
Apple Hard Disk 20 T-226
Apple Hard Disk 20SC T-9
Apple Hard Disk 40SC T-9
Apple Hard Disk 80SC T-9
Apple key T-38
Apple menu I-54, N85
Apple Numerics Manual P-xviii
Apple Personal Modem T-9
Apple Programmer's and Developer's
    Association (APDA) C-xvii, P-185,
    T-256
Apple Sound Chip (ASC) C1-3, T-142, 172,
    217, 222, 225
Apple symbol T-38, 232
Apple Tape Backup 40SC T-9
Apple technical documentation T-257
AppleLine 3270 File Transfer program T-180
AppleShare V-380, N114, N115, N116, T-9
    drop folders N165
    foreground applications N167
AppleShare File Server T-180
AppleTalk T-9, 116, 133, 134, 179, 228, 246
    address II-265, T-181
    architecture T-181
    drivers T-169, 176
AppleTalk Filing Protocol (AFP) V-523, T-183
    command mapping V-541

login command format V-543
read command format V-547
write command format V-545
AppleTalk Link Access Protocol II-263, T-183
assembly language II-306
data reception II-325
Pascal II-276
AppleTalk Manager I-13, II-261, 271, IV-229, V-507, N9, N20, N132, T-22, 38, 131, 181
assembly language II-304
high level N121
Pascal II-273
protocols T-181
AppleTalk PC card T-180
AppleTalk Session Protocol (ASP) V-522
AppleTalk system configurations V-519
AppleTalk Transaction Protocol II-266, 267, T-183
assembly language II-312
Pascal II-287
application T-26
files P-122, T-70
font I-219, T-106
number T-132
heap I-74, II-9, P-46, T-142
limit II-17, 29
zone T-145
list IV-243, T-129
parameters II-20
space II-20, T-142, 211
window I-270
mouse event handling in P-36
application-defined event T-39
applications, startup P-21 *See also* programs/programming
ApplicZone function II-32, N83
ApplLimit global variable II-19, 21, 29, IV-257
ApplScratch global variable I-85
ApplZone global variable II-19, 21, 32, N2, N83
AppParmHandle global variable II-57
Arabic Interface System T-111
/ARB3–/ARB0 C2-5, C5-2, 4, 5, 6, C6-2, 8
arbitration C5-2, C6
arbitration contest, defined C2-7
arbitration phase IV-286, T-175
arbitration signals C2-5
arithmetic drawing modes V-59
arithmetic operation T-184
ARPANET T-247
Arrow T-96

arrow cursor I-163, 167
arrow global variable I-147, 163
arrow keys IV-3, 57
/AS C13-9
ascent of a font I-228
in TextEdit I-378
ASCII T-40, 180, 247
codes I-247, T-43
keyboard input/printer output and P-164
ASPAbortOS function V-537
ASPCloseAll function V-538
ASPCloseSession function V-537
ASPGetParms function V-538
ASPGetStatus function V-540
ASPOpenSession function V-536
ASPUserCommand function V-539
ASPUserWrite function V-538
assembly language I-83, IV-13, V-3 *See also* MPW Assembler or specific version
asserted, defined C2-7
asynchronous communication II-245, T-177
asynchronous execution
AppleTalk Manager II-273
Device Manager II-180
File Manager II-97, IV-115
at-least-once transaction II-266
AtMenuBottom global variable V-249
ATP N9, N20
.ATP driver II-264, 267, 289, 315, IV-229
ATPAddRsp function II-295
ATPCloseSocket function II-291
ATPGetRequest function I-293, N20
ATPLoad function I-290, N20
ATPOpenSocket function II-290
ATPParamBlock packed record V-512
ATPReqCancel function II-293
ATPRequest function II-292
ATPResponse function II-296, N20
ATPRspCancel function II-296
ATPSndRequest function II-291
ATPSndRsp function II-294
ATPUnload function II-290
AttachPH function II-308, V-513
AttachVBL function V-567
attention cycle C3-10
defined C2-7
attention-null cycle C3-11
defined C2-7
attention-resource-lock cycle C3-11, C5-7
auto-key
event I-244, 246, P-34, T-37, 39, 43
rate I-246, II-371, T-43, 132

threshold I-246, II-371, T-43, 132
auto-pop bit I-89
automatic scrolling I-48
  in TextEdit I-380, IV-57
A/UX Operating System C1-6, T-190
  communications T-246
  document development applications T-246
  features T-238
  memory requirements T-241
  software development environment T-245
  system administration T-248
A/UX Toolbox T-243
AuxCtlHead global variable V-216
AuxCtlRec record V-217
AuxDCE packed record V-424
AuxWinHead global variable V-200
AuxWinList V-200
AuxWinRec record V-201

B

B*-tree IV-168
BackColor procedure I-174, N73
background procedure II-153
BackPat procedure I-167
BackPixPat procedure V-74
base line I-227, T-94, 108
baud rate II-246, 251, 254, T-177
BBU (Bob Bailey Unit) C12-4
BDSElement data type II-288
BDSPtr data type II-288
BDSType data type II-288
BeginUpdate procedure I-292, P-97, 167
Berkeley 4.2 BSD VAX implementation of PCC
    P-140
/BERR C1-9, C13-8
/BG C13-8
/BGACK C13-8
Binary-Decimal Conversion Package I-12, 487,
    IV-69, N90, T-21, 77
bit T-89
  image I-143, P-64, T-89
  manipulation I-470
  map N41, N117, T-91
    AppleTalk Manager II-268
    printing II-164
    QuickDraw I-144
  rate T-177
  structure (NuBus) C4-7

bit-mapped display T-82
bit-mapped graphics P-24, 62, 66
BitAnd function I-471
BitClr procedure I-471
BitMap data type I-144
BitMapType data type II-287
BitNot function I-471
BitOr function I-471
bits, reserved P-163
BitSet procedure I-471
BitShift function I-472
Bits16 data type I-146
BitTst function I-471
BitXor function I-471
black global variable I-162
blessed folder N20, N67
blind transfer T-227
block T-147
block (file) *See* allocation block
block contents II-10
block data transfers C3-12
block device II-175, T-167
block header II-10
  structure II-24
block map II-122, IV-162
Block Servers N20
blocks (of memory) I-73, II-10, P-45, 47 *See
    also* memory
  fragmentation of P-47, 49
  moving P-47
  obtaining P-51
  releasing P-51
BlockMove procedure II-44
'BNDL' resource N29, N48
'BNDL' cdev resource V-327
B-NET T-247
board sResource list V-437, C8-4, 17
BoardId C8-17
boot blocks N113, N134, T-160 *See also*
    system startup information
BootDrive N77
booting N124
boundary rectangle I-144, P-62
boundsRect P-161
/BR C13-8
break II-246
break/CTS N56
break table V-309
bridge II-265, T-181, 183
BringToFront procedure I-286
broadcast service II-264

BufPtr global variable II-19, 21, IV-257, N2, N14, N81
BufTgDate global variable II-212
BufTgFBkNum global variable II-212
BufTgFFlag global variable II-212
BufTgFNum global variable II-212
bug
  FCBRec N87
  LaserWriter ROMs N123
  QD clip regions N59
  SCSI N96
  TEScroll on Plus N22
  TextEdit N82, N131
BuildBDS function V-515
BuildDDPwds procedure V-514
BuildLAPwds procedure V-514
bundle II-85, III-11, N29, N48, T-128
  bit N48
  resource format III-12
bundling P-122
bus drivers and receivers C6-3
bus error T-189
bus interface unit (BIU) architecture C1-8
bus locking C5-6
  defined C2-7
bus parity signals C3-5
bus parking C5-9
bus timeout C3-10
bus transfer complete C3-10
bus-free phase IV-285, T-175
button T-20, 53, 54
  dimmed T-55
Button function I-259
button type of control I-311, 404
Byte data type I-78, C8-2
byte lane mapping C4-8
ByteLanes field C8-6
byte structure (NuBus) C4-7
byte swapping C4-7

C

C *See* MPW C or specific version
C Compiler P-140, T-245
C SANE Library P-140, 141
C8M C13-8
C16M C13-8
cache, 68020 N117-20 *See also* data caching

CacheCom N81
caching N81
CalcCMask procedure V-72
CalcMask procedure IV-24
CalcMenuSize procedure I-361
Calculator T-78
CalcVBehind procedure I-297
CalcVis procedure I-297
CalcVisBehind procedure I-297
calling a driver C9-7
canBackground N158
capacitance limits for a NuBus card C6-6
Caps Lock key P-34, T-40, 42, 43
card, defined C2-7
card-generic drivers C9-4
cards (Macintosh SE). *See also* disk controller
    card; Macintosh SE; SE-Bus expansion
    interface
  accessing electronics from C13-10
  accessing I/O devices from C13-10
  accessing RAM from C13-11
  connector C15-4, Foldout 4
  electrical design guide C13-2
  EMI guidelines for C13-18
  external connections for C15-2
  physical design guide for C14-2
cards (NuBus). *See also* disk controller card;
    Macintosh II; NuBus; NuBus Test Card;
    SCSI-NuBus Test Card; video card
  connector C7-3, Foldout 1
  connector shield Foldout 2
  driver design C9-2
  driver-supported C3-17
  electrical design guide C6-2
  EMI guidelines for C6-10
  firmware C8-2, 4
  96-pin plug connector for C7-3
  peer C3-17
  physical design guide C7-2, Foldout 1
  power control from C1-2, C6-3
card slot identification signals C3-2
card-specific drivers C9-3
caret I-376, 379
  blink time I-260, II-371, T-132
CaretTime global variable I-260
catalog tree file IV-171, T-161
CatMove function IV-157
caution alert P-106, 107, T-59
CautionAlert function I-420, V-284, P-109, 167
CCR N2
CCrsr record V-62

'cctb' resource V-221
'CDEF' resource V-221
cdevs V-324
  function V-329
  resource V-327, 329
cell IV-262, T-62
certified developer status P-157
CGrafPort record V-49, P-74
Chain procedure II-59, N52
ChangedResource procedure I-123
channel T-173
character
  codes I-246, T-40
    processing T-42
  device II-175, T-167
  image I-227, T-108
  keys I-33, 246, T-40, 42
  offset I-228
  origin I-228, T-108
  position I-375
  rectangle I-228, T-109
  set I-247, T-112
  style I-151, T-93
    of menu items I-348, 360
  width I-173, 228, T-109
CharByte function V-306
CharExtra procedure V-77
Chars data type I-384
CharsHandle data type I-384
CharsPtr data type I-384
Char2Pixel function V-308
CharType function V-306
CharWidth function I-173, N26, N82
check box I-312, 404, T-20, 34, 53, 54
  dimmed T-55
check exception T-189
check mark in a menu I-347, 358
Check Register Against Bounds (CHK)
    instruction T-189
CheckItem procedure I-358
CheckRslRecord N173
Checksumming N7
CheckUpdate function I-296
Chinese Interface System T-111
Chooser IV-216, T-26, 78, 130, 133, 228
  changes to V-428
  communication with IV-217
  operation of IV-219
  window T-133
  writing a driver to run under IV-221
chunky pixel image V-54
'cicn' resource V-65, V-78, V-80, P-88

CIcon record V-64
CInfoPBPtr data type IV-117
CInfoPBRec data type IV-125
CInfoType data type IV-117
Clascal environment P-140
class P-147
classic Macintosh T-2
Clear To Send (CTS) T-178
ClearMenuBar procedure I-354, V-247
click *See* mouse-down event
click loop routine I-380
  List Manager IV-266
  TextEdit IV-58
Clikloops N82
clikStuff N127
clip region N59
ClipAbove procedure I-296
Clipboard I-58, T-20, 26, 60, 63 *See also*
    scrap
clipping region of a grafPort I-149, 161, T-86
ClipRect procedure I-167
clipRgn of a grafPort I-149
/CLK C2-5, 6, C3-2, C6-8
clock chip, II-369, IV-251, T-131
  hardware III-36
clock rate P-163
clock signal C3-2
close box *See* go-away region
Close command I-56
Close function, high-level IV-112
  Device Manager II-178
  File Manager II-94
Close function, low-level IV-144
  Device Manager II-184
  File Manager II-114
close routine
  of a desk accessory I-446
  of a driver II-187, 193
CloseATPSkt function II-316, V-513
CloseCPort procedure V-68
closed device driver II-176, T-169
closed file II-83, IV-94, T-158
CloseDeskAcc procedure I-440
CloseDialog procedure I-413, P-107, 167
CloseDriver function II-178
ClosePgon procedure I-190
ClosePicture procedure I-189, P-86, 167
ClosePoly procedure I-190
ClosePort procedure I-164
CloseResFile procedure I-115, N116
CloseRgn procedure I-182, P-85, 167
CloseSkt function II-312, V-513

CloseWD function IV-158
CloseWindow procedure I-283, P-96, 98, 167
closing
   alerts P-107
   dialogs P-107
   edit record P-118
   files P-132
   windows P-95
ClrAppFiles procedure II-58
clump IV-124, 167
clump size IV-124, 167
'clut' resource V-78, 81, P-88
CMovePBPtr data type IV-117
CMovePBRec data type IV-127
CmpString function II-377
CMY color model V-43, 171
CMY2RGB procedure V-175
code, self modifying N117
CODE segment P-155, T-21
colon T-158
color V-14, T-100
   alerts P-106
   controls P-110
   dialogs P-106
   drawing I-158, 173
   menus V-227, P-105
   printing N73
   table V-46
      animation V-153
color description, in graphics port record P-73
color graphics port T-94
Color Look-Up Table (CLUT) V-46, 134, T-97
Color Manager, V-133, T-19, 101
   routines V-141
color model conversion routines V-174
Color Picker Package V-171, T-77, 100, 130,
   134
   dialog box T-135
   routines V-174
Color QuickDraw V-39, P-60, 87, T-83, 97, 99
   See also QuickDraw
   cursors and P-88
   graphics ports and P-74
   routines V-66
   text and P-88
Color Toolbox T-97
color wheel T-135
ColorBit procedure I-174
ColorInfo record V-159
coloring with CopyBits N163
ColorSpec record V-49, 136
ColorTable record V-48, 135

Color2Index function V-141
command files P-137
command phase IV-286, T-175
Command symbol T-38
Command-C T-47
Command-= T-47
Command-key P-34, T-40, 43, 46, 62, 123,
   129, 232
   combination *See* keyboard equivalent
   equivalent *See* keyboard equivalent
Command-period II-154
Command-+ T-47
Command-Shift-number I-258, T-38, 47
Command-Shift-1 T-47
Command-Shift-2 T-47
Command-V T-47
Command-X T-47
Command-Z T-47
commands I-51, 341
compacting T-148
compaction, heap I-74, II-12, 39
CompactMem function II-39, N51
compatibility P-8, 160
   future machines N2, N117
   guidelines IV-xii, V-1
   HFS N44
   large-screen displays N100
   Standard File N47
completion routine
   Device Manager II-180, 181
   File Manager II-97, 99, IV-115
   Sound Driver II-231
compliance categories C3-17
CompProc procedure V-147
configuration files N115
ConfirmName function II-323, V-513
connector drawings C7-3, C14-6, 9
   electrical description of NuBus C6-2
   electrical description of SE-Bus C13-2
connector pin assignments C6-5, C11-18,
   C13-2
content region of a window I-271, P-92, T-51
context dependence T-112
control T-20, 34, 48, 53
   highlighted T-55
   inactive T-55
control character T-42
control color table V-218
control definition function I-314, 328, IV-53,
   V-220, T-54
control definition ID I-315, 328
Control function

high-level II-179
low-level II-186
Control key V-21
Control Manager I-11, 309, IV-53, V-215,
    P-110, 112, T-20, 48, 53, 97
  routines I-319, IV-53, V-221
Control Panel V-323, T-43, 59, 78, 122, 130,
    185, 210, 233
control record I-316
control routine C9-14
  of a desk accessory I-446
  of a driver II-187, 194
control signals C2-5, C3-4
control template I-315, T-54
  resource format I-332
ControlHandle data type I-317
ControlPtr data type I-317
ControlRecord data type I-317
controls I-65, 311, P-110
  color in P-110
  defining your own I-328, P-112
  in a dialog/alert I-404
  information II-176
  modifying P-113
  multiple lines of text in IV-53
  part codes for P-111
  removing P-112
coordinate origin T-88
coordinate plane I-138, T-87
coordinate systems, graphics ports and P-75
Copy T-47, 63
copy protection N117, P-163
CopyBits procedure I-188, V-70, N41, N55,
    N120, N163
CopyMask procedure IV-24, V-71
CopyPixMap procedure V-70
CopyPixPat procedure V-73
CopyRgn procedure I-183
CouldAlert procedure I-420, V-285
CouldDialog procedure I-415, V-284
Count1Resources function IV-15
Count1Types function IV-15
CountADBs function V-369
CountAppFiles procedure II-57
CountMItems function I-361
CountResources function I-118
CountTypes function I-117
courteous colors V-154
CProcRec record V-146
CPUFlag variable V-348, N2
CQDProcs record V-91
CRC field C8-7

Create function
  high-level II-90, IV-112
  low-level II-107, IV-145
CreateResFile procedure I-114, N101
creators P-125, T-126, 158
creator of a file III-9
'crsr' resource V-63, 78, P-88
CrsrThresh global variable II-372
cSpecArray V-49, 136
cString data type C8-2
CTab2Palette procedure V-165
CtlCTab record V-218
CurActivate global variable I-280
CurApName global variable II-58
CurApRefNum global variable II-58
CurDeactive global variable I-280
CurDirStore global variable IV-72, N80
CurJTOffset global variable II-62
CurMap global variable I-117
CurPageOption global variable II-60
CurPitch global variable II-226, 232
current directory button IV-72
current heap zone II-10, 31
current limits for a NuBus card C6-6
current resource file I-105, 116
CurrentA5 global variable I-95, II-19, 21, 386
    N25, N136
CurResFile function I-116
CursHandle data type I-474
cursor I-146, T-46, 95, 186
  Color QuickDraw and P-88
  data type I-146
  level I-167, P-84
  QuickDraw routines I-167, P-84
  standard cursors I-147, 474
  utility routines I-474
CursPtr data type I-474
CurStackBase global variable II-19, 21, 358
'CUST' resource N135
customizing ancestors P-147
Cut T-47, 63
cut and paste I-59, T-63
  in TextEdit I-385
  intelligent I-63
CWindowRecord V-199
cycle (NuBus), defined C2-7

D

D0–D15 C13-9
DABeeper global variable I-411
dangling pointers I-75
DAStrings global array I-421
data caching C3-17
data cycle, defined C2-8
data bits II-245, T-177
data buffer II-83, 176, IV-95, T-158
data fork I-105, II-81, IV-93, P-122, T-68, 154
data frame T-183
data mark II-211
data phase IV-286, T-176
Data Servers N20
Data Terminal Ready line IV-225, 248
data transfer (NuBus) C3-2
   timing C6-7
data types I-86, C8-2
datagram II-265, T-183
   loss recovery II-268
Datagram Delivery Protocol II-265, N9, T-183
   assembly language II-308
   Pascal II-281
date operations II-377
date/time record II-377
DateForm data type I-504
DateTimeRec data type II-378
Date2Secs procedure II-379
dBoxProc P-92
DC specifications for line drive (NuBus card)
      C6-2
'dctb' resource V-278
DCtlEntry data type II-190
DCtlHandle data type II-190
DCtlPtr data type II-190
DDP *See* Datagram Delivery Protocol
DDPCloseSocket function II-282
DDPOpenSocket function II-282
DDPRdCancel function II-284
DDPRead function II-283
DDPWrite function II-283
dead key T-43
debugger, Macintosh Plus ROM N38
debugger, FKEY N145
debugging N7, N51
declaration ROM V-437, C8-2, C9-4, 6, 11,
      T-210
Dec2Str N90, P-139, 151
default button T-56
   In a dialog I-67, 400, 407
   In an alert I-69, 401, 424
default directory IV-100
default error message T-190
default volume II-80, IV-100
   getting *See* GetVol function
   setting *See* SetVol function
Defense Data Network T-247
deferred printing T-115
Deferred Task Manager V-465
   routine V-467
DeferredTask record V-466
definition procedure T-36
DefltStack global variable II-17
DefOSRec record V-355
DefStartRec V-353
DefVCBPtr global variable II-126, IV-178
DefVideoRec V-354
delay N2, P-164
Delay procedure II-384
DelComp procedure V-147
Delete function
   high-level II-97, IV-113
   low-level II-119, IV-147
DeleteMenu procedure I-354, V-244, P-103,
      104, 167
DelMCEntries procedure V-238
DelMenuItem procedure IV-56, V-244
DelSearch procedure V-147
DeltaPoint function I-475
Dequeue function II-383
dereferencing a handle II-14, P-46
DeRez P-140, T-80
derived font T-104
descendants P-147
descent of a font I-228
Designing Cards and Drivers for the Macintosh II
      and Macintosh SE P-xviii
desk accessory I-437, N1, N5, N23, P-5, T-20,
      26, 47, 130, 169
   out-of-memory conditions and P-57
   window, mouse event handling in P-35
   writing your own I-443
Desk Manager I-12, 435, T-20, 39, 169
   routines I-440
desk scrap I-453, IV-61, T-60, 63
   data types I-454
   format I-462
   routines I-457
DeskHook global variable I-282, 288
DeskPattern global variable I-282
desktop I-32, 269, T-34
   interface T-34

Desktop file   III-10, IV-243, N29, N48, T-124, 127, 129
destination rectangle   I-374, P-116
DetachPH function   II-308, V-513
DetachResource procedure   I-120
Developer Services (Apple)   P-157
development tools   P-136
device   II-175, T-167
Device Address   V-366
device control entry   II-189, IV-215
device driver   I-13, II-175, N56, T-22, 168
   event   I-244, T-38, 39
   for a desk accessory   I-443
   structure   II-187
   writing your own   II-193
device handler ID   V-365
device information, in graphics port record   P-68
device ID   IV-217
device I/O
   Macintosh SE   C12-6
   Macintosh II   C1-5
Device Manager   I-13, II-173, IV-213, V-421, T-22, 168, 189
   routines   II-177, V-427
      device control entry access   II-189
      for writing drivers   II-194
      high-level   II-178
      low-level   II-180
device package   IV-217
device partition map   IV-292
device resource file   T-133
Device Servers   N20
DeviceList   V-118
diaeresis   T-158
dial   I-312, T-54
dialog box   I-66, 399, P-105, T-14, 47, 53, 56
   Close   IV-10
   closing   P-107
   creating your own   IV-74
   color in   P-106
   editing text in   P-110
   handling events in   P-107
   opening   P-107
   types of   P-106
dialog color table   V-278
dialog filter   N34
dialog hook   N47
dialog item list   V-279
Dialog Manager   I-12, 397, IV-59, V-277, P-105, 107, T-20, 48, 54, 56, 97, 188
   routines   I-411, IV-59, V-283
dialog pointer   I-407

dialog record   I-403, 407, T-57
dialog template   I-402, 403, T-57
   resource format   I-425
dialog window   I-401
dialogs, modeless   N5
DialogPeek data type   I-408
DialogPtr data type   I-407
DialogRecord data type   I-408
DialogSelect function   I-417, N34, P-108, 168
DialogTemplate data type   I-423
DialogTHndl data type   I-424
DialogTPtr data type   I-424
DIBadMount function   II-396, N70, P-34, 168
DiffRgn procedure   I-184
DIFormat function   II-398
DILoad procedure   II-396
dimmed
   control   I-313
   menu item   I-342, 343
   menu title   I-342
DInfo data type   IV-105
DirCreate function   IV-146
direct devices   V-134
directory   IV-89, T-155
   ID   IV-92
   name   IV-90
   record   IV-172
DirectoryOffset field   C8-8
dirID   N77
disabled
   dialog/alert item   I-405
   menu   I-342, 358
   menu item   I-349, 358
DisableItem procedure   I-358, V-245, P-104, 168
Discipline   N117
discontinuous selection   I-40
disk controller card (for Macintosh SE)   C16-2.
   See also cards (Macintosh SE); Macintosh SE
   address allocation   C16-9
   block diagram   C16-3
   bus control signals   C16-5
   device select decode addresses   C16-9
   DMA operations   C16-8
   Macintosh SE interface logic   C16-5
   PIO timing   C16-7
   system configuration   C16-2
disk controller card (for Macintosh II)   C10-15.
   See also cards (NuBus); Macintosh II; NuBus
   block diagram   C10-17

device select decode addresses C10-20
DMA operations C16-8
memory map and the declaration ROM C10-20
NuBus interface logic C10-18
RAM access signals C10-18
system configuration C10-15
disk drive T-159, 227
Disk Driver I-13, II-209, IV-223, V-469, T-22, 160, 163, 169, 226
advanced Control calls IV-223
Device Manager calls II-213
routines II-214
Disk Initialization Package I-13, II-393, IV-239, N70, T-23, 77, 154, 157, 162
routines II-396
disk-inserted event I-244, P-34, T-37, 39, 186
event message I-252
responding to I-257
disk interface III-33, T-226
disk speed controller T-142
disk-switch dialog II-80, T-159
DiskEject function II-214
dispatch table *See* trap dispatch table
display rectangle I-406
display routines P-60 *See also* Color QuickDraw; QuickDraw
display screen T-167
DispMCInfo procedure V-239
DisposCCursor procedure V-75
DisposCIcon procedure V-76
DisposControl procedure I-321
DisposCTable procedure V-78
DisposDialog procedure I-415
DisposeDialog P-107, 168
DisposeControl procedure I-321, P-168
DisposeMenu procedure I-352, P-103, 168
DisposePalette procedure V-162
DisposeRgn procedure I-182
DisposeWindow procedure I-284, P-96, 98, 168
DisposGDevice function V-123
DisposHandle procedure I-76, 80, II-33, N8, P-51, 168
DisposMenu procedure I-352
DisposPixMap procedure V-70
DisposPixPat procedure V-73
DisposPtr procedure I-75, 79, II-36, P-51, 169
DisposRgn procedure I-182
DisposWindow procedure I-284
dithering V-57
'DITL' cdev resource V-327
'DITL' resource V-278

DIUnload procedure II-396
DIVerify function II-398
divide instruction T-189
DIZero function II-399, N70
dkGray global variable I-162
DlgCopy procedure I-418, P-110
DlgCut procedure I-418, P-110
DlgDelete procedure I-418, P-110
DlgFont global variable I-412
DlgHook function IV-75
SFGetFile I-526
SFPutFile I-522
DlgPaste procedure I-418, P-110
'DLOG' resource V-278
DMA C12-6
DMA Acknowledge signal IV-252
DoCaret N82
document files P-122, T-71
document window I-269, 279, T-48
overlapping T-50
regions and frame T-52
Documentor's Workbench (DWB 2.0) T-246
documentProc P-92
DoDraw N82
double-click I-37, 255
double-click time I-260, II-371, T-132
DoubleTime global variable I-260
DoVBLTask function V-568
dQDrvSize N36
draft printing II-151, 153, T-115
DraftBits N128
drag delay V-24
drag region of a window I-271, 289, P-92, T-51
DragControl procedure I-325
DragGrayRgn function I-294, V-209
DragHook global variable
Control Manager I-324, 326
Window Manager I-295
DragPattern global variable
Control Manager I-324, 326
Window Manager I-288, 289, 290, 295
DragTheRgn function I-295
DragWindow procedure I-289, P-98, 169
DRAM *See* Dynamic RAM chips
dRAMBased N71
DrawChar procedure I-172, N26, P-83, 169
DrawControls procedure I-322, P-169
DrawDialog procedure I-418
DrawGrowIcon procedure I-287, P-169
drawing I-155
color I-158, 173
DrawJust procedure V-310

DrawMenuBar procedure   I-354, V-244, P-101, 104, 169
DrawNew procedure   I-296
Draw1Control procedure   IV-53
DrawPicture procedure   I-190, N21, N35, N59, P-86, 169
DrawString procedure   I-172, N26, P-83, 170
DrawText procedure   I-172, P-83, 170
Drive button   T-157
drive, defined   C2-8
drive number   II-80, IV-93, T-159
drive queue   II-127, IV-181, N36, T-159
driver descriptor map   IV-292
driver I/O queue   II-180, 191
driver name   II-176
driver reference number   II-176
driver-supported cards   C3-17
drivers   N71 *See also* device driver
  calling   C9-7
  card-generic   C9-4
  card-specific   C9-3
  design of   C9-2
  installing at startup   C9-5
  video   C9-10
drives, foreign   N28
DriveStatus function   II-215
driving edge, defined   C2-8
DrvQEl data type   II-127, IV-181, N36
DrvQHdr global variable   II-128, IV-182
DrvrInstall   N108
DrvrRemove   N108
DrvSts data type   II-215
DSAlertRect global variable   II-362
DSAlertTab global variable   II-359, 362
DSErrCode global variable   II-362
/DTACK   C13-9
DTInstall function   V-467
DTR   *See* Data Terminal Ready line
DXInfo data type   IV-106
Dynamic RAM chips   IV-246

E

E clock   C13-8
Echo Protocol (EP)   V-522
echoer   V-522
echoer socket   V-522
Edit menu   I-58
  and desk accessories   I-441, 447

edit record   I-374, P-115
  closing/opening   P-118
editing text in dialogs   P-110
'EFNT' resource   N84
800K disk   T-163
800K floppy disk drive   T-227
800K volume   T-160, 162
Eject function
  high-level   II-90, IV-108
  low-level   II-107, IV-135
ejection, premature   N106
electrical design guide
  for Macintosh SE cards   C13-2
  for NuBus cards   C6-2
electrical schematic
  NuBus Test Card   Foldout 3
  SCSI-NuBus Test Card   C10-14
Elementary Functions Package   T-184
Elems68K   *See* Transcendental Functions Package
Elems881   N146
ellipsis   T-45
EMI guidelines
  for external connections (Macintosh SE)   C15-3
  for Macintosh SE cards   C13-18
  for NuBus cards   C6-10
empty handle   I-76, II-14, 40
EmptyHandle procedure   II-40
EmptyRect function   I-176
EmptyRgn function   I-186
enabled
  dialog/alert item   I-405
  menu   I-358
  menu item   I-358
EnableItem procedure   I-358, V-245, P-104, 170
end-of-file   II-81, IV-93
End-of-line   N127
end-of-message flag   II-270
EndUpdate procedure   I-293, P-97, 170
Enqueue procedure   II-382
Enter key   T-56
entity name   II-265, 298
EntityName data type   II-298
EntityPtr data type   II-298
Environs procedure   II-385, IV-236
equal-tempered scale   II-237
EqualPt function   I-193
EqualRect function   I-176
EqualRgn function   I-185
EqualString function   II-377
EraseArc procedure   I-180

EraseOval procedure I-178
ErasePoly procedure I-192
EraseRect procedure I-177
EraseRgn procedure I-186
EraseRoundRect procedure I-179
error C3-10
error codes III-205, V-572, P-40, 129, 162
error number *See* result code
error reporting
    Memory Manager IV-80
    Resource Manager IV-18
ErrorSound procedure I-411
Escape key V-21
'ETAB' resource N84
EtherTalk T-180, 247
event I-243, T-19, 27, 36
    code I-249
    mask I-253, T-37
    message I-249
    posted T-36
    priority I-245, T-39
    record I-249, T-38
    system T-39
    types I-244, T-37
event-driven programming P-7, T-27, 29, 36
Event Manager, Operating System I-13, II-65,
        IV-85, P-30
    routines II-68, IV-85
Event Manager, Toolbox I-11, 241
    routines I-257
event masking P-39
event queue I-243, P-39, T-36, 40
    structure II-70
event recording *see* journaling mechanism
EventAvail function I-259
EventQueue global variable II-71
EventRecord data type I-249
events/event loop P-30, 107 *See also* specific
        event type
EvQEl data type II-71
exactly-once transaction II-266
example program I-13
exception II-195, N2, T-217
exception vector III-17, T-141
exclusive-OR T-86
ExitToShell procedure II-59, N64
expansion cards. *See* cards
expansion connector. *See* connector
expansion slot T-209
explicit colors V-156
exponential functions II-407
/EXT.DTK C13-8

Extended Protocol Package (XPP) driver V-524
extended selection I-39
    In TextEdit I-384
extent IV-170
    descriptor IV-171
    record IV-171
extents tree file IV-170, T-161
external connections, for Macintosh SE cards
        C15-2
external file system II-128, IV-182
external reference I-95
ExtStsDT global variable II-199

F

family character-width table IV-39
family number IV-30
family record IV-36
family resource IV-43
family style-property table IV-38
FamRec data type IV-36
FCB *See* file control block
FCBPBPtr data type IV-117
FCBPBRec data type IV-179
FCBSPtr global variable II-127, IV-179
'FCMT' resource N29
'fctb' resource V-183, 184
FC0–FC2 C13-8
FdFlags N40
Fedit T-160
Fetch function II-194
Fetch procedure N-178
FFComment N29
FFSynthPtr data type II-228
FFSynthRec data type II-228, N19
FHeaderRec packed record V-449
fields (of objects) P-144
53C80 SCSI C1-3
5380 SCSI C12-4
file II-79, 81, IV-89, 93, P-122, T-68, 154
    access modes V-376, P-130, T-158
    assumptions about a P-162
    catalog *See* hierarchical file directory
    closing P-132
    command P-137
    creating P-131
    creator III-9
    directory II-79, 122, IV-89
    extent T-161

filter   N47
I/O queue   II-97, 124, IV-115, 175
Icon   II-85, III-10, IV-105
   menu   I-55
   name   II-81, IV-90, N107
   number   II-122, IV-163
   object   T-129
   opening   P-131
   reading from   P-131
   record   IV-172
   reference   III-10, T-128
      resource format   III-12
   source   P-139
   system   N24, N44, N66, N94, N102
   tags   II-212
      buffer   II-212
   type   III-9, P-124, T-126, 127, 158
   writing to   P-132
file control block   II-126, IV-94, 178, N102,
   T-158, 161
   buffer   T-161
File Manager   I-13, II-77, IV-89, P-124, 129,
   T-16, 22, 39, 124, 154, 158, 168, 189,
   226
   alert   T-190
   routines
      for queue access   II-125, 126, 128, IV-176,
         178, 181
      high-level   II-88, IV-106
      low-level   II-97, IV-115
File Manager extensions   V-375
File menu   P-125
File Open dialog box   P-126
File Save dialog box   P-128
File Servers   N20
file-control-block buffer   II-126, IV-178
fileFilter function   I-524
filename   T-158
FillArc procedure   I-181
FillCArc procedure   V-69
FillCOval procedure   V-69
FillCPoly procedure   V-69
FillCRect procedure   V-69
FillCRgn procedure   V-69
FillCRoundRect procedure   V-69
FillOval procedure   I-178
FillPoly procedure   I-192
FillRect procedure   I-177, P-80, 170
FillRgn procedure   I-187
FillRoundRect procedure   I-179
filterProc function   I-415
financial functions   II-407

FindControl function   I-323, P-98, 114, 170
FindDItem function   IV-60, N112
Finder   N114, N116, P-21, T-15, 26, 122, 124,
   135, 159, 161, 166
   default icon   T-128
   flags   N40
   information   II-55, IV-104, T-116, 126, 127,
      151
   interface   II-55, 84, III-7, IV-243
   screen   T-124
Finder-related resources   III-10
FinderName global variable   II-59
FindWindow function   I-287, P-35, 114, 170
FindWindow procedure   V-208
FindWord procedure   V-309
FInfo data type   II-84, IV-104
FInitQueue procedure   II-103, IV-128
firmware (NuBus card)   C8-2
   sample code   C8-20
FixATan2 function   IV-65
FixDiv function   IV-64
Fixed data type   I-79
fixed devices   V-134
fixed-point
   arithmetic   I-467
   numbers   I-79
fixed-width font   I-228, T-109
FixMul function   I-467
FixRatio function   I-467
FixRound function   I-467
Fix2Frac function   IV-65
Fix2Long function   IV-65
Fix2SmallFract function   V-175
Fix2X function   IV-65
'FKEY' resource   N3
FlashMenuBar procedure   I-361, V-246
flat file directory   IV-89, 163, T-156
flat file system   T-155
Floating-Point Arithmetic and Transcendental
   Functions Packages   V-595
Floating-Point Arithmetic Package   I-13, II-403,
   T-23, 77, 184
floating-point error   T-190
floating-point operation   T-208
Flush command   V-363, 364
FlushEvents procedure   II-69, P-31, 170
FlushFile function   II-114, IV-144
FlushVol function   P-132, 133
   high-level   II-89, IV-108
   low-level   II-105, IV-133
FMetric data type   IV-32
FMInput data type   I-224

FMOutPtr data type I-227
FMOutput data type I-227
FMSwapFont function I-223
FmtDefaults global variable IV-241
'FOBJ' resource N29
folder II-85, IV-105, T-155
'FOND' resource IV-29, V-181, 185
font T-69, 78, 93, 102
font association table IV-38, T-105
font characterization table I-225
Font/DA Mover IV-31, N6, N23, T-77, 103, 105
Font Manager I-11, 215, IV-27, V-179, T-19, 72, 102, 187
  communication with QuickDraw I-224, IV-33
  data structures IV-34
  routines I-222, IV-31, V-180
Font menu I-60, 353
'FONT' resource IV-29, 44, V-181, N30
fonts I-60, 151, 217, IV-29, N92
  characters I-220
  family IV-29, T-104
  format I-227
  height I-228, T-109
  number I-217, 219, IV-30, T-102
  QuickDraw and P-82
  record I-230, IV-35
  rectangle I-228
  resource IV-42, T-104
    format I-234
    ID I-234
  scaling I-220, IV-33, T-104, 106, 119
  script V-298
  size I-153, 217, T-103
    variable IV-56
FontInfo data type I-173
FontMetrics procedure IV-32
FontRec data type I-231
FontScript function V-314
FontSize menu I-61
Font2Script function V-315
ForeColor procedure I-173, N73
fork I-105, II-81, IV-93, T-68
format block V-437, C8-4, 5
Format field C8-7
formatting hierarchical volumes IV-240
Fortran T-245
Fortran-77 T-245
400K disk T-163
400K volume T-162
four-tone record II-227

four-tone synthesizer II-223, 226, T-170, 172
FPMove N137
FP68K *See* Floating-Point Arithmetic Package
FracCos function IV-64
FracDiv function IV-64
FracMul function IV-64
FracSin function IV-64
FracSqrt function IV-64
Fract type IV-63
FractEnable global variable IV-32, N72, N92
fractional character widths IV-33, T-104, 107
fractional pen positioning V-84
Frac2Fix function IV-65
Frac2X function IV-65
fragmentation N39, P-47, 49
frame T-177
  ALAP II-264
  check sequence II-265
  header II-264
  picture I-158
  pointer (stack) I-96
  serial communication II-246
  stack I-96, II-17
  trailer II-264
  window I-271
FrameArc procedure I-180
FrameOval procedure I-177
FramePoly procedure I-192
FrameRect procedure I-176
FrameRgn procedure I-186
FrameRoundRect procedure I-178
framing error II-246
free block T-147
free memory block II-10
free-form synthesizer II-223, 228, T-170, 172
free-form wave T-171
FreeAlert procedure I-420, V-285
FreeDialog procedure I-415, V-284
FreeMem function II-38
FreeWave data type II-228
'FREF' cdev resource V-327
'FREF' resource N29, N48
frequency II-223, T-171
FrontWindow function I-286
FScaleDisable global variable I-222, IV-32, N92
FSClose function II-94, IV-112, P-132, 133, 171
FSCreate P-131, 171
FSDelete function II-97, IV-113
FSFCBLen global variable IV-97, N66
FSOpen function II-91, IV-109, P-131, 171

FSQHdr global variable   II-125, IV-176
FSRead function   IV-109, P-131, 171
   Device Manager   II-178
   File Manager   II-92
FSWrite function   IV-110, P-132, 171
   Device Manager   II-179
   File Manager   II-92
ftp   T-247
FTSndRecPtr data type   II-227
FTSoundRec data type   II-227
FTSynthPtr data type   II-227
FTSynthRec data type   II-227
full pathname   IV-99
full-duplex communication   II-245, T-177
function keys   V-22
FXInfo data type   IV-105

G

gamma table   C9-16
GDevice record   V-119
General cdev   V-325
Get Info   T-159
Get1IndResource function   IV-15
Get1IndType procedure   IV-15
Get1NamedResource function   IV-15
Get1Resource function   IV-16
GetADBInfo function   V-369
GetAlrtStage function   I-422
GetAppFiles procedure   II-58, N77
GetAppFont function   V-315
GetApplLimit function   II-29
GetAppParms procedure   II-58
GetAuxCtl function   V-222
GetAuxWin function   V-207
GetBackColor procedure   V-68
GetBridgeAddress function   V-515, N132
GetCaretTime function   I-260
GetCatInfo function   IV-155
GetCCursor function   V-75, P-88, 171
GetCIcon function   V-76
GetClip procedure   I-167
GetColor function   V-174
GetCPixel procedure   V-69
GetCRefCon function   I-327
GetCTable function   V-77
GetCTitle procedure   I-321
GetCtlAction function   I-328
GetCtlMax function   I-327

GetCtlMin function   I-327
GetCtlValue function   I-326, P-114, 171
GetCTSeed function   V-143
GetCursor function   I-474, P-84, 171
GetCVariant function   V-222
GetCWMgrPort procedure   V-205, 210
GetDateTime procedure   II-378
GetDblTime function   I-260
GetDCtlEntry function   II-190
GetDefaultStartup procedure   V-353
GetDefFontSize function   V-315
GetDeviceList function   V-124
GetDItem procedure   I-421
GetDrvQHdr function   II-128, IV-181
GetEntryColor procedure   V-164
GetEntryUsage procedure   V-165
GetEnvirons function   V-313
GetEOF function   P-132, 172
   high-level   II-93, IV-111
   low-level   II-112, IV-142
GetEvQHdr function   II-71
GetFCBInfo function   IV-179
GetFileInfo function
   high-level   II-95, IV-113
   low-level   II-115, IV-148
GetFInfo function   II-95, IV-113
GetFName procedure   I-223
GetFNum procedure   I-223
GetFontInfo procedure   I-173, P-83, 172
GetFontName procedure   I-223
GetForeColor procedure   V-68
GetFPos function   P-132
   high-level   II-92, IV-110
   low-level   II-111, IV-141
GetFSQHdr function   II-125, IV-175
GetGDevice function   V-123
GetGrayRgn function   V-208
GetHandleSize function   II-33
GetIcon function   I-473, P-83, 172
GetIndADB function   V-369
GetIndPattern procedure   I-473, P-81
GetIndResource function   I-118
GetIndString procedure   I-468
GetIndType procedure   I-117
GetItem procedure   I-358, P-104, 172
GetItemCmd procedure   V-240
GetItemIcon procedure   I-360, V-246
GetItemMark procedure   I-359, V-246
GetItemStyle procedure   I-360, V-247
GetIText procedure   I-422, N18
GetItmIcon procedure   I-360
GetItmMark procedure   I-359

GetItmStyle procedure I-360
GetKeys procedure I-259
GetMainDevice function V-124
GetMaskTable function IV-25
GetMaxCtl function I-327
GetMaxDevice function V-125
GetMBarHeight function V-315
GetMCEntry function V-239
GetMCInfo function V-239
GetMenu function I-351, V-243, N78, P-102, 172
GetMenuBar function I-355, P-172
GetMHandle function I-361, V-246
GetMinCtl function I-327
GetMMUMode function V-592
GetMouse procedure I-259
GetNamedResource function I-119
GetNewControl function I-321, P-112, 113, 114, 172
GetNewCWindow function V-207
GetNewDialog function I-413, V-284, N4, P-107, 172
GetNewMBar function I-354, V-247, P-102, 172
GetNewPalette function V-162
GetNewWindow function I-283, P-95, 173
GetNextDevice function V-124
GetNextEvent function I-257, N3, N5, N85, P-30, 32, 34, 39, 40, 97, 108, 173
GetNodeAddress function II-303
GetOSDefault procedure V-355
GetOSEvent function II-69, N85
GetPalette function V-163
GetPattern function I-473, P-81, 173
GetPen procedure I-169, P-78, 173
GetPenState procedure I-169, P-78, 173
GetPicture function I-475, P-86, 173
GetPixel function I-195
GetPixPat function V-73
GetPort procedure I-165, P-63, 67, 97, 173
GetPtrSize function II-37
GetRequest function II-317, V-513
GetResAttrs function I-121
GetResFileAttrs function I-113, 127
GetResInfo procedure I-113, 121
GetResource function I-119, P-173
GetRMenu function I-351
GetRslData operation N173
GetScrap function I-459
GetScript function V-312
GetSoundVol procedure II-232
GetString function I-468

GetStylHandle function V-268
GetStylScrap function V-268
GetSubTable procedure V-142
GetSysFont function V-315
GetSysJust function V-315
GetSysPPtr function II-381
GetTime procedure II-380
GetTimeout procedure V-356
GetTrapAddress function II-384, IV-234, N2
GetVBLQHdr function II-352
GetVCBQHdr function II-126, IV-178
GetVideoDefault procedure V-354
GetVInfo function II-89, IV-107, N157
GetVol function N77, N140
    high-level II-89, IV-107
    low-level II-104, IV-131
GetVolInfo function
    high-level II-89, IV-107
    low-level II-104, IV-129
GetVRefNum function II-89, IV-107
GetWDInfo function IV-159
GetWindowPic function I-293
GetWMgrPort procedure I-282
GetWRefCon function I-293
GetWTitle procedure I-284
GetWVariant function V-208
GetZone function II-31
GhostWindow global variable I-287
global coordinates I-155, P-77
global variables P-161, T-7
    list III-227, IV-309, V-607
    QuickDraw I-138, 162
global width table IV-41
GlobalToLocal procedure I-193, P-77, 110, 174
go-away region of a window I-271, 288, P-92, T-51
GrafDevice procedure I-165
GrafPort data type I-148
grafPort I-147, P-62, T-91, 114, 215 *See also* graphics ports
    coordinate system I-153
    regions T-92
    routines I-162
GrafPtr data type I-148
GrafVars record V-67
GrafVerb data type I-198
Grand Funnel P-7
GRANT C5-4, 6
graphic resources I-147
graphics, bit-mapped P-24, 62, 66
graphics devices V-117, 118
    routines V-122

graphics pen T-93, 108
graphics ports P-62, 67, T-51, 86, 91
    Color QuickDraw and P-74
    coordinate systems and P-75
graphics routines P-60 *See also* Color
    QuickDraw; QuickDraw
gray global variable I-162
GrayRgn global variable I-282, 296, V-121,
    205
grow image of a window I-289, T-51
grow region of a window I-272, 289, P-93
grow zone function II-14, 42, N136, T-149
GrowWindow function I-289, V-209, P-98, 174
GZRootHnd global variable II-43
GZSaveHnd function II-43

H

/HALT C13-8
HandAndHand function II-375
handle I-75, 78, II-12, N155, P-45, T-36, 72,
    149
    data type I-78
    dereferencing II-14
    empty II-40
    fake N117
    manipulation II-374
    nil N7, N117
HandleZone function II-34
HandToHand function II-374
Hard Disk 20 IV-223
    crashing N134
hardware III-15, IV-245
    Macintosh SE C12-2
    Macintosh II C1-2
hardware overrun error II-246, T-178
HClrRBit procedure IV-79, N2
HCreate function IV-146
HDelete function IV-147
heap I-12, 23, II-9, 17, C12-5, P-46, T-21, 145
    compaction I-74, II-12, 39
    creating on the stack II-45
    reserved P-58
    space T-147
heap zone II-9, 22, V-3, T-145
HeapEnd global variable II-19, 21
heat dissipation guidelines
    Macintosh SE C14-9
    Macintosh II C7-4

Hebrew Interface System T-111
height table N30
HFS *see* hierarchical file system
HFSDispatch trap macro IV-118
HGetFileInfo function IV-149
HGetState function IV-79, N2
HGetVInfo function IV-130
HGetVol function IV-132
HideControl procedure I-322, P-113, 114, 174
HideCursor procedure I-168, P-84, 174
HideDItem procedure IV-59
HidePen procedure I-168
HideWindow procedure I-283
hierarchical file directory IV-89, T-156
hierarchical file system (HFS) IV-89, N44, N66,
    N68, N77, T-155
hierarchical menu V-226, T-45 *See also*
    menus/menu items
hierarchical volume T-161
high, defined C2-8
highlighting I-31, T-49, 55
    control I-313
    menu title I-357
    window I-270
HiliteColor procedure V-77
HiliteControl procedure I-322
HiliteMenu procedure I-357, V-245
HiliteMode global variable V-61
HiliteRGB global variable V-62
HiliteText procedure V-310
HiliteWindow procedure I-286
HiWord function I-472
HLock procedure II-41, N2
HLS color model V-43, 171
HNoPurge procedure II-42, N2
HomeResFile function I-117
HOpen function IV-136
HOpenRF function IV-137
horizontal blanking interval III-18
hotSpot I-146, P-84, T-96
HParamBlkPtr data type IV-117
HParamBlockRec record V-390
HParmBlockRec data type IV-118
    FileParam variant IV-122
    IOParam variant IV-120
    VolumeParam variant IV-123
HPurge procedure II-41
HRename function IV-154
HRstFLock function IV-152
HSetFileInfo function IV-150
HSetFLock function IV-151
HSetRBit procedure IV-79, N2

HSetState procedure IV-80, N2
HSetVol function IV-133
HSetVolInfo function IV-131
HSL2RGB procedure V-175
HSV color model V-43, 171
HSV2RGB procedure V-175
Human Interface Guidelines P-xviii
HUnlock procedure II-41, N2
HyperCard P-149
  background field limit N169
  background printing N168
  closeField N169
  dial N169
  exit to N169
  file format N170
  find command N169
  idle handler N169
  MultiFinder and N169
  private access N169
  'snd ' resource and N168
  title bar highlighting N169
  visual effect N169
  word wrap N169
HyperTalk P-150

I

'ICN#' resource N29, N48, N55
'ICN#' cdev resource V-327
icon I-32, N55-1, T-14, 69, 78, 95
  for a file II-85, III-10
  in a dialog/alert I-404
  in a menu I-347, 359
    number I-347
  QuickDraw and P-83
  utility routines I-473
icon list III-11, T-128
  resource format I-476, III-12
'ictb' resource V-278
ID code C2-5, C2-9
ID=33 N151
/ID3–/ID0 C2-5, C3-2, C5-4
illegal instruction T-189
image width I-228, T-109
ImageWriter N3, N33, T-9, 26, 114, 115, 133,
  241, 246
ImageWriter II T-9
ImageWriter, AT N124

IMMED N2, N44
immediate printing T-115
inactive
  defined C2-8
  control I-313
  window I-46, 270
include file T-25
indexing IV-101
Index2Color procedure V-141
indicator of a dial I-312
InfoScrap function I-457
inheritance, objects and P-145
Init procedure N178
'INIT' resource N110
'INIT' 31 resource IV-256, V-352
InitAllPacks procedure I-484
InitApplZone procedure II-28
InitCPort procedure V-67
InitCursor procedure I-167, P-84, 174
InitDialogs procedure I-411, P-107, 112, 174
InitFonts procedure I-222, P-31, 95, 101, 107,
  112, 118, 174
InitGDevice procedure V-122
InitGraf procedure I-162, P-31, 63, 95, 101,
  107, 112, 118, 174
initialization resources IV-256, T-78, 79
initiator device IV-285, T-175
InitMenus procedure I-351, V-242, P-101, 107,
  175
InitPack procedure I-484
InitPalettes procedure V-161
InitPort procedure I-164
InitPRAMRecs function V-454
InitProcMenu procedure V-238
InitQueue procedure II-103, IV-128
InitResources function I-114
InitSDeclMgr function V-451
InitsRsrcTable function V-453
InitUtil function II-380
InitWindows procedure I-281, V-208, P-31, 78,
  95, 101, 107, 112, 118, 175
InitZone procedure II-29
input driver II-246, T-177
insertion point I-41, 375, IV-4
InsertMenu procedure I-353, V-243, P-98, 102,
  104, 175
InsertResMenu procedure I-353, V-243
InsetRect procedure I-175
InsetRgn procedure I-184
Inside Macintosh P-xvi, xviii, 154
InsMenuItem procedure IV-55
InsNewItem procedure V-243

Installer   N75, T-77
installing a driver at startup C9-5
InsTime procedure IV-300
Institute of Electrical and Electronics Engineers
      (IEEE) C1-3
Intel 8021 microprocessor T-230
interface file T-25
interface routine I-95
international resources I-495
International Standards Organization (ISO) T-
      111
International Utilities Package   I-12, 493, V-9,
      287, P-27, T-21, 77
   routines I-504
   sorting routines V-291
internet II-265, N9, T-181
   address II-265, 314, T-181
interrupt II-195, N85-1, T-217
   level-1 (VIA) II-197, III-38
   level-2 (SCC) II-198
   level-3 II-196
   vertical retrace II-349
interrupt handler II-195, T-217
   writing your own II-200
interrupt priority level II-196
interrupt signal T-234
interrupt tasks V-466
interrupt vector II-196
interrupts, slot device C9-8
'INTL' resources N153
'INTL' 0 resource V-288
'INTL' 1 resource V-288
'INTL' 2 resource V-288
Intl0Hndl data type I-496
Intl0Ptr data type I-496
Intl0Rec data type I-497
Intl1Hndl data type I-500
Intl1Ptr data type I-500
Intl1Rec data type I-500
IntlScript function V-314
intrinsic font T-104
IntlSpec global variable IV-42
Int64Bit data type I-472
InvalRect procedure I-291
InvalRgn procedure I-291
InverRect procedure I-177
InverRgn procedure I-186
InverRoundRect procedure I-179
inverse table V-137
InvertArc procedure I-181
InvertColor procedure V-141
InvertOval procedure I-178

InvertPoly procedure I-192
InvertRect procedure I-177, P-80, 175
InvertRgn procedure I-186
InvertRoundRect procedure I-179
invisible
   control I-316
   dialog/alert item I-406
   file icon II-85
   window I-274
I/O connector shield C7-5, Foldout 2
I/O device T-216
   accessing from cards C13-10
I/O queue *See* driver I/O queue or file I/O queue
I/O request II-97, 180, IV-115
I/O system error T-189
ioACAccess record V-388
ioActCount N19
ioACUser record V-390
ioCompletion N130
ioDenyModes record V-389
ioDirID N77
IODone function II-195
ioFCBIndx N87
ioFDirIndex N69
ioFlFndrInfo N40
ioFlNum N77
ioFlVersNum N102
ioNamePtr N179
ioObjType record V-388
ioVDRefNum N106
ioVDrvInfo N106
ioVFndrInfo N67
ioWDProcID N77
/IPL0–/IPL2 C13-8
IsATPOpen function II-304
IsDialogEvent function I-416, N5, P-108, 175
IsMPPOpen function II-304
ITab record V-139
item T-57
   dialog/alert I-403
   menu I-341
   type I-404
item list I-403, T-57
   resource format I-427
item number
   dialog/alert I-406
   menu I-350
'itl ' resources N153
'itl0' resource V-288
'itl1' resource V-288
'itl2' resource V-288
'itlb' resource V-288, N160

'itlc' resource V-288
IUCompString function I-506, N58
IUDatePString procedure I-505
IUDateString procedure I-504
IUEqualString function I-506, N58
IUGetIntl function I-505
IUMagIDString function I-507, N58
IUMagString function I-506, N58
IUMetric function I-505
IUStrData N178
IUSetIntl procedure I-506
IUTimePString procedure I-505
IUTimeString procedure I-505
IWM (Integrated Woz Machine) III-17, C1-3,
    C12-4, N2, T-192, 216, 226
IWM global variable III-34

J

JADBProc variable V-367
Japanese Interface System T-111
jDoVBLTask V-568
jDTInstall V-467
JFetch global variable II-194
jGNEFilter N85
JIODone global variable II-195
job dialog II-149
job subrecord II-150
journal code I-262
JournalFlag global variable I-261
journaling mechanism I-261, T-37
JournalRef global variable I-261
JStash global variable II-195
jump table II-60, T-142, 151
jump vector II-194
just-tempered scale II-237
justification I-376, T-112
    gap V-305
    setting I-387

K

KanjiTalk N138, T-111
KbdLast variable V-367
KbdType variable V-367
'KCHR' resource V-190, N160

kernel T-242
kerning I-152, 228, T-94, 109
kerning table IV-40
Key Caps T-26, 78, 110
key codes I-250, T-43
Key Mapping N160
key script V-298
key-down event I-244, T-37, 39, 40, 43
    responding to I-256
key-down transitions IV-250
key-up event I-244, 254, T-37, 39, 40
keyboard I-33, IV-250, V-190, T-229
    configuration I-248
    equivalent I-343, P-103, T-46, 47
        meta-character I-348
        responding to I-356
        standard equivalents I-53, IV-74
        reserved IV-7
    event I-244, 246, P-34, T-37, 40
        event message I-250, V-193
        responding to I-256
    hardware III-29
    input, ASCII and P-164
    mapping procedure T-42
    mapping resource T-78
    touch *See* auto-key threshold
Keyboard cdev V-325
KeyMap data type I-260
keypad I-35, IV-250
    hardware III-29
KeyRepThresh global variable I-246
KeyScript procedure V-314
KeyThresh global variable I-246
KeyTrans function V-195, N160
KillControls procedure I-321, P-113, 175
KillGetReq function V-514
KillIO function
    high-level II-179
    low-level II-187
KillNBP function V-514
KillPicture procedure I-190
KillPoly procedure I-191
KillSendReq function V-514
'KMAP' resource V-190, N160

L

LActivate procedure IV-276
LAddColumn function IV-271

LAddRow function IV-271
LAddToCell procedure IV-272
LAP N9
LAPAdrBlock data type II-276
LAPCloseProtocol function II-277
LAPOpenProtocol function II-277
LAPRdCancel function II-279
LAPRead function II-278
LAPWrite function II-277
Laser Prep N152
LaserShare N133, T-116
  Print Spooler T-180
LaserWriter N21, N72, T-9, 26, 87, 104, 107,
    114, 117, 133, 179, 241, 246
  fonts T-118
LaserWriter Plus T-9, 117
  fonts T-118
Launch N52, N126, T-244
  procedure II-60
LAutoScroll procedure IV-275
LCellSize procedure IV-273
LClick function IV-273
LClrCell procedure IV-272
LDelColumn procedure IV-271
LDelRow procedure IV-272
LDispose procedure IV-271
LDoDraw procedure IV-275
LDraw procedure IV-275
/LDS C13-9
leading I-228, T-103
Length field C8-7
LFind procedure IV-274
LGetCell procedure IV-272
LGetSelect function IV-273
LHElement V-263
LHTable V-263
library file T-25
ligatures I-501
line P-79, 87, 175
  breaks N92
  height I-378
  layout N92
  QuickDraw and P-78
line drive (NuBus card), DC and AC
    specifications for C6-2
Line procedure I-171
line 1010 exception T-189
line 1111 exception T-189
LineTo procedure I-170, P-79, 87, 175
'LINK' resource N88
linker T-151
Lisa Clascal environment P-140

Lisa Pascal N2, P-140
list IV-261, T-61
  cell selection IV-266
  defining your own IV-262, 276
  drawing IV-262
  element IV-261, T-61
list definition procedure T-62
List Manager Package IV-259, T-21, 61, 77,
    134
  routines IV-269
list record IV-262
list separator I-497
Listen command V-363, 364
ListHandle data type IV-264
ListPtr data type IV-264
ListRec data type IV-263
LLastClick function IV-273
LNew function IV-270
LNextCell function IV-274
loading segments P-56
LoadNBP function II-324
LoadResource procedure I-119
LoadScrap function I-458
LoadSeg procedure II-60, IV-83, N43
local coordinates I-153, P-76
local ID III-10
localization V-8, V-294, P-26, T-110
LocalToGlobal procedure I-193, P-77, 176
location (of screen) P-161
location table I-231
lock bit II-25
locked
  block I-76, II-10, T-147
  file II-84, IV-94, T-159
  volume II-80, IV-93, T-159
locking C5-6
locking a block I-76, II-41
LockRng function IV-138
LodeScrap function I-458
logarithmic functions II-407
logical
  block II-119, IV-89, 160, T-160
  end-of-file II-81, IV-93
  size of a block II-22
logical operations I-471
logical state definitions C6-2
long data type C8-2
LongMul procedure I-472
Long2Fix function IV-65
LookupName function II-323, V-513
Lo3Bytes global variable I-85, II-25

low, defined C2-8
lowercase T-76, 158
low-memory globals N117
LoWord function I-472
LRect procedure IV-274
LScroll procedure IV-275
LSearch function IV-274
LSetCell procedure IV-272
LSetSelect procedure IV-273
LSize procedure IV-274
ltGray global variable I-162
LUpdate procedure IV-275
Lvl1DT global variable II-197
Lvl2DT global variable II-198

M

MacApp P-141
　introduction to P-148
　Object Pascal and P-147
　programming in P-149
　sample programs and P-156
MacDraw T-63
'mach' cdev resource V-327, 328
Macintosh
　character set T-41
　classic T-2
　hardware/software relationship T-7
　overview of P-2
　software architecture of P-12
Macintosh Family Hardware Reference P-xviii
Macintosh 512K T-2
Macintosh 512K enhanced T-2, 16
Macintosh II N117, T-5, 16, 198 *See also*
　cards (NuBus); NuBus
　address allocations C4-5
　architecture C1-2
　block diagram C1-4, T-219, 221
　Color Toolbox T-98
　disk controller card for C10-15
　expansion slots T-209
　floating-point coprocessor T-207
　hardware T-200
　hardware compatibility T-9
　I/O T-201
　Keyboard V-190, 191
　memory management T-206
　power supply T-7
　RAM T-140

sound chip T-225
　specifications T-254
　video T-216
　　card for C11-2
Macintosh II to NuBus address mapping C4-5
Macintosh Interface Libraries P-140, 141
Macintosh Plus T-2, 3, 194
　block diagram T-217
　display screen T-167
　hardware compatibility T-9
　keyboard V-190, 191, T-230
　power supply T-7
　RAM T-140
　ROM debugger N38
　sound T-223
　specifications T-251
Macintosh Programmer's Workshop *See* MPW
Macintosh Programmer's Workshop 2.0
　　Reference P-xviii *See also* MPW
Macintosh ROM T-14
Macintosh SE N117, T-4, 16, 196 *See also*
　　cards (Macintosh SE); SE-Bus expansion
　　interface
　accessing electronics from an expansion card
　　C13-10
　additional support for expansion C12-7
　address space C13-16
　architecture C12-2
　　block diagram C12-3, T-219, 220
　disk controller card for C16-2
　display screen T-167
　expansion connector T-208
　hardware T-200
　hardware compatibility T-9
　power supply T-7
　RAM T-140
　sound T-223
　specifications T-252
MacPaint N3, T-26
　document format N86
Macsbug N7, N113, P-139, 151
MacWrite T-128
magnitude of a wave II-223, T-171
mail T-247
main event loop I-16, T-29 *See also*
　events/event loop
main screen V-121
main segment II-55, P-55, T-150
MainDevice global variable V-124
MajorBaseOS C8-16
MajorLength C8-16
makefiles P-139

MakeITable procedure V-142
MakeRGBPat procedure V-73
manager T-15
MapPoly procedure I-197
MapPt procedure I-196
MapRect procedure I-196
MapRgn procedure I-196
mark P-129
  in a file II-82, IV-94
  in a menu I-347, 359
mark state II-245
masks, defined P-39
master, defined C2-8
master directory block II-120, IV-160
master pointer I-75, II-12, N7, T-150
  allocation II-22, 31
  structure II-25
MatchRec record V-71
MaxApplZone procedure II-30, IV-77, 83,
    N39, N103
MaxBlock function IV-77
MaxMem function II-38
MaxSizeRsrc function IV-16
MBarEnable global variable I-356, 446
MBarHeight global variable V-253, N117
MBarHook global variable I-356
'MBDF' resources V-250
MC68000 microprocessor C12-4, N146, T-5,
    25, 141, 189, 192, 202
  address space T-203
  expansion connector T-208
  functional description of signals C13-8
MC68020 microprocessor C1-3, T-25, 172,
    200, 202
  address space T-204
MC68851 Paged Memory Management Unit
    (PMMU) T-206
MC68881 floating-point numerics processor
    C1-3, T-184, 207, 240
MCEntry V-231
MCTable V-232
'mctb' resource V-234
'MDEF' resources V-248, P-100
MDEF procedure, message 3 N172
MDS Edit N84
MeasureJust procedure V-311
MeasureText procedure IV-25
MemErr global variable IV-80, N7
MemError function II-44, N7
memory P-42, T-211 *See also* blocks
  block I-73, II-10
  elements of P-44

management of II-7, P-46, T-144
  introduction I-71
organization of II-19, IV-257, P-42
out-of-memory conditions and P-568
parking garage analogy P-43
reorganization of P-52
segment loader and P-53
system use of P-52
Memory Manager I-12, II-7, IV-77, P-42,
    T-21, 73, 140, 145, 187
  routines II-27, IV-77
memory, routines that may move or purge III-
    211, IV-303, V-601
MemTop global variable II-19, 21, 44
menu I-341, P-99, T-14, 20, 34, 44, 69
  accessing/changing P-104
  blink T-132
  color in P-105
  defining your own I-362
  definition procedure I-344, 362, IV-56,
    V-248, P-100, T-44
  disabled T-45
  features V-24
  guidelines I-51
  highlighting V-235
  item I-341, T-45
    blinking I-361, II-371
    entry V-234
    number I-350
  list I-345, P-102
  record I-344
  removing P-101
  resource format I-364, P-100
  scrolling IV-56
  setting up P-101
  standard menus I-54, 342
  title I-341
    entry V-233
menu bar I-341, T-20, 44, 47
  definition procedure V-250
  defproc messages V-251
  entry V-233
  mouse event handling in P-36
  resource format I-365
menu color information table V-231
menu ID I-344
Menu Manager I-12, 339, IV-55, V-225, P-99,
    T-20, 44, 45, 72, 97
  using P-101
  routines I-351, IV-55, V-238
MenuChoice function V-240, P-103, 105, 176
MenuCInfo global variable V-242

MenuCRsrc V-234
MenuDisable global variable V-249
MenuFlash global variable I-361
MenuHandle data type I-345
MenuHook global variable I-356
MenuInfo V-230
    data type I-345
MenuKey function I-356, V-245, P-105, 176
MenuList global variable I-346, V-228, N85
MenuPtr data type I-345
MenuSelect function I-355, V-244, P-36, 103,
    105, 176
message P-147
message phase IV-286, T-176
meta-characters
    AppleTalk Manager II-266, 320
    Menu Manager I-346
methods, defined P-142
Microsoft Word T-180
MIDI (Musical Instrument Digital Interface) V-
    475, 496, T173
MIDI synthesizer V-475, T-173
Mini-8 connector IV-248
MiniFinder T-125
MinorBaseOS C8-16
MinorLength C8-16
MinStack global variable II-17
MinusOne global variable I-85
miscellaneous exception T-189
missing symbol I-152, 220, 230, T-94, 106
MMU32Bit global variable V-592, N2
modal dialog box I-67, 400, 415, P-106, T-56,
    59
ModalDialog procedure I-415, N34, P-108,
    176
mode, 24/32 bit C1-6, C4-3
modeless dialog box I-67, 400, 416, P-106,
    T-57
modem T-229
    port configuration T-131
modes I-28
modifier T-174
modifier flag I-252
    structure V-194
modifier keys I-34, 246, P-34, T-40, 42
    lags in event record I-252
ModifierStub record V-482
modifying controls P-113
modulo C3-6
monitor cables N144
Monitors cdev V-325
MoreMasters procedure II-31, N53

Motorola MC68xxx *See* MC68xxx
mounted volume II-79, IV-92, P-122, T-158
MountVol function IV-128
mouse I-36, T-233
    hardware III-25
    location I-259, 323
    scaling II-372
    windows and P-97
Mouse cdev V-325
mouse event handling P-33, 35
    mouse-down event I-244, T-29, 37, 39
        responding to I-255
    mouse-up event I-244, T-37, 39
        responding to I-255
mouse scaling T-132, 233
    threshold T-233
mouse-tracking resource T-78
Move procedure I-170, P-79, 176
MoveControl procedure I-325, P-113, 176
MoveHHi procedure II-44, IV-77, 83, N103,
    N111
MovePortTo procedure I-166
MoveTo procedure I-170, P-79, 177
MoveWindow procedure I-289, V-209, P-177
moving blocks P-47
MPNT N86
mPopupMsg, MDEF message N172
MPP II-271
.MPP driver II-264, 271, IV-229
MPPClose function II-275
MPPOpen function II-275
MPPParamBlock packed record V-511, 551
MPW T-26, 80, 158, 245
    Assembler P-141
    C P-140, N164, N166
    described P-136
    Linker N110
    Pascal P-140
    sample programs and P-156
    Shell P-139, T-242
MPW:%_InitObj file N105
MPW:%_MethTables file N93, N105
MPW:Globals/Assy file N104
MPW:Linker file N93
MPW:Object Pascal file N105
MPW:_DataInit file N93
MPW:{$LOAD} file N93
multibit fonts V-83
MultiFinder N158, N177, N180, T-27, 39,
    125, 166
    screen T-125
multiple screens V-121

multitasking T-206, 238
Munger function I-468
Musical Instrument Digital Interface (MIDI) V-475, 496, T-173
MyCallBack procedure V-480
MyModifier function V-480

N

name lookup II-266
Name-Binding Protocol II-266, N9, T-183
   assembly language II-319
   Pascal II-298
names directory II-266
names information socket II-266
names table II-266, 321
NBP See Name-Binding Protocol
NBP tuple II-266
NBPConfirm function II-301, N9
NBPExtract function II-300
NBPExtract function V-515
NBPLoad function II-301
NBPLookup function II-300, N9, N20
NBPRegister function II-299, N20
NBPRemove function II-301
NBPSetEntity procedure V-514
NBPSetNTE procedure V-515
NBPUnload function II-301
negZcbFreeErr N151
network event I-244, II-275, T-38, 39
Network File System (NFS) T-247
network number II-265
networkEvt N142
network-visible entity II-265, T-181
New command I-56
NewCDialog function V-283
NewControl function I-319, P-112, 114, 177
NewCWindow function V-207
NewDialog function I-412, P-107, 177
NewEmptyHandle function IV-78
NewGDevice function V-122
NewHandle function I-76, 80, II-32, N7, N117, P-51, 177
newline character II-84, IV-95
newline mode II-84, IV-95
NewMenu function I-351, P-102, 103
NewPalette function V-161
NewPixMap function V-70
NewPixPat function V-72

NewPtr function I-75, 79, II-36, P-51, 177
NewRgn function I-181, P-85, 177
NewString function I-468
NewWindow function I-282, P-95, 178
'NFNT' resource IV-30, V-181, 183
NGetTrapAddress function IV-234, N156
Nil pointers P-165
96-pin connector
   Macintosh SE and C14-6
   Macintosh II and C7-3
/NMRQ C2-4, 5, C3-3, 11, C6-2
node II-263, T-179
   ID II-263
noErr P-40, 129
noGrowDocProc P-92
non-aligned MC68020 access C3-16
non-aligned reads C3-16
non-aligned writes C3-16
nonblind transfer T-227
nonbreaking space I-246
non-master request C3-3
nonrelocatable block I-75, II-10, P-47, T-147
   allocating II-36
   out-of-memory conditions and P-57
   releasing II-36
note alert P-106, 107, T-59
note synthesizer V-475, T-173
NoteAlert function I-420, V-284, P-109, 178
'nrct' cdev resource V-327
'nrct' resource V-329
NSendRequest function V-514
NSetTrapAddress procedure IV-234
nsvErr N24
NuBus T-5, 209 *See also* cards (NuBus); Macintosh II
   address space C4-3
   arbitration C5-2
   bit and byte structure C4-7
   block read transaction C3-13
   block write transaction C3-14
   connector pin assignments C6-5
   data transfer C3-2
   definitions C2-7
   design examples C10-2
   implementation rules C3-11
   interface architecture C1-8
   interrupt mechanism C3-11
   interrupt operations C3-11
   licensing requirements CI-4
   overview C2-2
   power budget C6-6
   read transaction C3-7

slot address space T-142
system clock C2-6
write transaction C3-8
NuBus Test Card C10-2. *See also* cards
    (NuBus); Macintosh II; NuBus; SCSI-
    NuBus Test Card
  byte swapping and C10-4
  electrical schematic C Foldout 3
  hardware organization C10-6
  master operation C10-9
  master register interpretation C10-3
  master transaction timing C10-8
  overview of operation C10-2
  PAL listings for CA-1
  programming C10-5
  programming model (registers) C10-2
  register addresses C10-3
  slave operation C10-9
NuBus to Macintosh II address mapping C4-5
NuBus to processor bus state machines C1-9
null event I-245, T-38, 40
nulls N107
NullSTRec V-264
numeric formatter IV-69
numeric scanner IV-69
NumToString procedure I-489

O

object-oriented programming P-141
Object Pascal P-140, 146
  MacApp and P-147
objects
  defined P-142, 143
  fields of P-144
  inheritance and P-145
ObscureCursor procedure I-168, P-84, 178
obtaining blocks P-51
off-line volume II-80, IV-92, T-159
OffLine function II-106, IV-134
offscreen bitmap V-125, N41
offscreen devices V-125
off-screen drawing T-86
offset data type C8-2
offset/width table I-231, IV-34
OffsetPoly procedure I-191
OffsetRect procedure I-174
OffsetRgn procedure I-183
offspring, of a directory IV-91

OfsetRgn procedure I-183
OldContent global variable I-296
OldStructure global variable I-296
on-line volume II-80, IV-92, T-159
OneOne global variable I-85
OpColor procedure V-77
Open Apple symbol T-38, 232
open collector, defined C2-8
Open command I-56, N102, T-126, 157
open device driver II-176, T-169
open file II-83, IV-94, T-158
Open function
  high-level IV-109
    Device Manager II-178
    File Manager II-91
  low-level IV-135
    Device Manager II-184
    File Manager II-108
open permission II-83, IV-95
open routine
  of a desk accessory I-445
  of a driver II-187, 193
OpenATPSkt function II-315, V-513
OpenCPort procedure V-67
OpenDeskAcc function I-440
OpenDriver function II-178
opening
  alerts P-107
  dialogs P-107
  edit record P-118
  files P-131
  windows P-95
OpenPicture function I-189, V-96, P-86, 178
OpenPoly function I-190
OpenPort procedure I-163
OpenResFile function I-115, N46, N78, N101
OpenRF function N74
  high-level II-91, IV-109
  low-level II-109, IV-137
OpenRFPerm function IV-17, N116
OpenRgn procedure I-181, P-85, 178
OpenSkt function II-311, V-513
OpenSlot function V-425
OpenWD function IV-158
Operating System I-9, P-20, T-6, 7, 14, 21,
    · 166
  calls P-166
  components T-17
  layers T-167
  queues II-372
Operating System Event Manager I-13, II-65,
    IV-85, T-21, 28, 36, 40, 229

routines II-68
Operating System Utilities I-13, II-367, IV-233, V-591
   routines II-374, IV-233, V-592, T-23
Option key P-34, T-40, 43, 43, 123, 129
OSErr data type II-373, P-129, 162
OSEventAvail function II-70
OSType data type II-373
output driver II-246, T-177
out-of-memory conditions P-56
   handling P-58
overrun error *See* hardware overrun error *or* software overrun error
owned resources I-109, N6

P

'PACK' resource IV-67
Pack 0 *See* List Manager Package
Pack 2 *See* Disk Initialization Package
Pack 3 *See* Standard File Package
Pack 4 *See* Floating-Point Arithmetic Package
Pack 5 *See* Transcendental Functions Package
Pack 6 *See* International Utilities Package
Pack 7 *See* Binary-Decimal Conversion Package
Pack12 *See* Color Picker Package
Package Manager I-12, 481, IV-67, T-20
packages I-12, 483, IV-67, T-20, 23
PackBits procedure I-470, N86
page T-206
page fault T-206
page rectangle II-150
Page Setup command I-57
Paged Memory Management Unit (PMMU) C1-6, T-206
PaintArc procedure I-180
PaintBehind procedure I-297
PaintOne procedure I-296, V-208
PaintOval procedure I-178
PaintPoly procedure I-192
PaintRect procedure I-177, P-80, 178
PaintRgn procedure I-186
PaintRoundRect procedure I-179
PaintWhite global variable I-297
PAL listings
   for NuBus Test Card CA-1
   for SCSI-NuBus Test Card CB-1
palette I-32, V-152
   customization V-158

prioritization V-157
   resource example V-160
Palette Manager V-151, T-19
   routines V-161
Palette record V-159
Palette2CTab procedure V-166
pane I-49
panel I-50
paper rectangle II-150
ParamBlkType data type II-98, 181, IV-117
ParamBlockRec data type II-98, 181, IV-118
   driver I/O queue entry II-191
   file I/O queue entry II-124, IV-175
   FileParam variant IV-122
   IOParam variant IV-120
   VolumeParam variant IV-123
parameter block I-93, II-97, 180, IV-116
parameter RAM II-369, IV-251, T-106, 130, 222
   default values II-370
   routines II-380
   settings T-131
ParamText procedure I-421
parent directory IV-91
parent ID IV-92
parity bit II-245, T-177
parity error II-246, T-177
parity signals C2-5, C3-5
parked, defined C2-8
ParmBlkPtr data type II-98, 181, IV-117
part code I-315, 330, P-111
partial pathname IV-99
partition map entry V-579
Pascal *See* MPW Pascal or specific version
Pascal data types, sizes of I-86
Pascal stack management T-145
Paste T-47, 63
pasting T-63
'PAT ' resource P-81
patch T-79
path reference number II-83, IV-94
PatHandle data type I-473
pathname IV-99, T-158
PatPtr data type I-473
pattern I-145, 473, N86, T-95
   QuickDraw and P-81
Pattern data type I-146
pattern list I-473
   resource format I-476
pattern-printing control, in graphics port record P-74
pattern transfer mode I-157

PBAllocate function II-113, IV-143
PBAllocContig function IV-143
PBCatMove function IV-157
PBClose function IV-144
  Device Manager II-184
  File Manager II-114
PBCloseWD function IV-158
PBControl function II-186
PBCreate function II-107, IV-145
PBDelete function II-119, IV-147
PBDirCreate function IV-146
PBEject function II-107, IV-135
PBFlushFile function II-114, IV-144
PBFlushVol function II-105, IV-133
PBGetCatInfo function IV-155, V-391, N68,
  N69
PBGetEOF function II-112, IV-142
PBGetFCBInfo function IV-179, N87
PBGetFInfo function II-115, IV-148, N24, N68
PBGetFPos function II-111, IV-141
PBGetVInfo function II-104, IV-129, N24,
  N44, N157
PBGetVol function II-104, IV-131
PBGetWDInfo function IV-159, N77
PBHCopyFile function V-396
PBHCreate function IV-146
PBHDelete function IV-147
PBHGetDirAccess function V-394
PBHGetFInfo function IV-149
PBHGetLogInInfo function V-393
PBHGetVInfo function IV-130, N66, N67, N77
PBHGetVol function IV-132
PBHGetVolParms function V-392
PBHMapID function V-395
PBHMapName function V-395
PBHMoveRename function V-397
PBHOpen function IV-136
PBHOpenDeny function V-398
PBHOpenRF function IV-137
PBHOpenRFDeny function V-398
PBHRename function IV-154
PBHRstFLock function IV-152
PBHSetDirAccess function V-394
PBHSetFInfo function IV-150
PBHSetFLock function IV-151
PBHSetVol function IV-133, N140
PBKillIO function II-187
PBLockRange function IV-138
PBMountVol function II-103, IV-128
PBOffLine function II-106, IV-134
PBOpen function IV-135
  Device Manager II-184

File Manager II-108
PBOpenRF function II-109, IV-137
PBOpenWD function IV-158, N77
PBRead function IV-139
  Device Manager II-185
  File Manager II-110
PBRename function II-118, IV-153
PBRstFLock function II-117, IV-152
PBSetCatInfo function IV-156
PBSetEOF function II-112, IV-142
PBSetFInfo function II-116, IV-150
PBSetFLock function II-116, IV-151
PBSetFPos function II-111, IV-141
PBSetFVers function II-117, IV-153
PBSetVInfo function IV-131
PBSetVol function II-105, IV-132
PBStatus function II-186
PBUnlockRange function IV-139
PBUnmountVol function II-106, IV-134
PBWrite function IV-140
  Device Manager II-185
  File Manager II-110
peer cards C3-17
pen characteristics I-150
pen description, in graphics port record P-69
PenMode procedure I-169, P-79, 178
PenNormal procedure I-170, P-79, 179
PenPat procedure I-170, P-79, 179
PenPixPat procedure V-74
pens, QuickDraw and P-78
PenSize procedure I-169, P-79, 179
PenState data type I-169
period, defined C2-8
period of a wave II-223, T-171
/PFW C2-5, C3-3, C6-2
  interaction with the power supply (NuBus card)
  C6-4
phase of a wave cycle II-223, T-171
physical design guide
  for Macintosh SE cards C14-2
  for NuBus cards C7-2
physical end-of-file II-81, IV-93
physical size of a block II-23
PicComment procedure I-189, N72, N91
picComments V-94
PicHandle data type I-159
PicPtr data type I-159
'PICT' data type I-455, P-86
PICT file V-85
  sample V-95
PICT opcodes V-96
  expanded format V-103

picture I-158, N21, T-87, 95
　comments I-159, N91, T-87
　　lines N91
　　polygons N91
　　printing forms N91
　　rotation N91
　　text N91
　compatibility V-92
　frame I-158, T-87
　QuickDraw routines I-189, P-86
　structures V-92
　utility routine I-475
Picture data type I-159
Picture record V-86
picture spooling V-87
　sample programs V-88, 89
pinouts N10, N65
PinRect function I-293
pixel I-139, 143, V-42, T-88
　images P-65, T-90
　maps P-66, T-91
　pattern V-55, P-81
　value V-42, T-101
Pixel2Char function V-307
PixMap record V-52, N120, N163
PixPat record V-55
PKillGetReq function V-518
PKillNBP function V-518
PKillSendReq function V-517
plainDBox P-92
PlotCIcon procedure V-76
PlotIcon procedure I-473, P-83, 179
'pltt' resource V-152
PmBackColor procedure V-163
/PMCYC C13-9
PmForeColor procedure V-163
PMSP N69, N77, N101
PNSendRequest function V-516
PNTG N86
point T-88, 103
point (coordinate plane) I-139
　routines I-193
Point data type I-139
point (font size) I-61, 153, 217
pointer T-36, 95, 149
　(on screen) I-36, 37 *See also* cursor
　(to memory) I-75, 78, II-11, N155, P-45
　　data type C8-2
　　manipulation II-374
　　nil N117
　　type coercion I-79
points, defined P-72

PollRoutine C9-10
polygon I-159, T-87
　routines I-190
　QuickDraw and P-87
Polygon data type I-159
PolyHandle data type I-160
PolyPtr data type I-160
pop-up menu V-25, T-47
PopUpMenuSelect function V-241, N156
port T-86
port description, in graphics port record P-69
Portable C Compiler (PCC) P-140
portBits of a grafPort I-148
PortBUse global variable II-305
portRect of a grafPort I-149
PortSize procedure I-165
post an event I-243
'POST' resource N91
PostEvent function II-68
posting alerts P-109
PostScript N72, N91, T-87, 117, 180
power budget
　Macintosh SE C13-19
　NuBus C6-6
power fail warning C3-3
power/ground signals C2-5
power supply (NuBus card)
　/PFW interaction with C6-4
　specifications C6-6
'ppat' resource V-78, 79, P-81, 88
PRAMInitData C8-1
PrClose procedure II-157, V-408, N161
PrCloseDoc procedure II-160, V-408
PrClosePage procedure II-160, V-408, N72
PrCtlCall procedure II-163, V-408
PrDlgMain N95
PrDrvrClose procedure II-163, V-408
PrDrvrDCE function II-163, V-408
PrDrvrOpen procedure II-163, V-408
PrDrvrVers function II-163, V-408
preflighting P-58
'PRER' resource IV-216
PrError function II-161, V-408, N72, N118
'PRES' resource IV-216
PrGeneral procedure V-410, N128
PrGlue trap V-408, 409
PrIdle procedure N118
primary ordering V-291
PrimaryInit C8-18
prime routine of a driver II-187, 193
PrimeTime procedure IV-300
Print Action routine N174

Print command   I-57, T-126
print dialogs   II-148, N95, T-115, 116
print record   II-148
PrintDefault procedure   II-158, V-408
printer
   low level calls   N124
   information subrecord   II-150
   output, ASCII and   P-164
   resource file   II-147
Printer Access Protocol (PAP)   T-183
printer connection   T-132
Printer Driver   I-13, II-147, 162, T-22, 26, 113,
      169, 176
printer font   T-118
printer port configuration   T-131
printer resource file   T-113
PrintErr global variable   II-161
printing   N118, T-113
   character   T-40
   color   N73
   device independent   N122
   doc names   N149
   LaserWriter   N72
   methods   II-153, T-115
      low-level   II-164
   spool/print-a-page   N125
printing grafPort   II-147, T-114
Printing Manager   I-13, II-145, V-407, P-23,
      164, T-113
   routines   II-157
printing resource   T-26
private scraps   I-461
privilege violation   T-189
PrJobDialog function   II-158, V-408
PrJobInit function   N95
PrJobMerge procedure   II-159, V-408
procedure-oriented programming   P-142
processor bus to NuBus state machine   C1-9
processor priority   II-196
ProcPtr data type   I-78
product safety
   Macintosh SE   C14-10
   Macintosh II   C7-5
programming seminars   P-156
programs/programming *See also* applications
   event-driven   P-7
   key ideas   P-5
   object-oriented   P-141
   procedure-oriented   P-142
   sample   P-139, 156
   segment loader and   P-53
   "taking apart"   P-156

types of   P-5
Project procedure   N178
PrOpen procedure   II-157, V-408, N161
PrOpenDoc function   II-159, V-408
PrOpenPage procedure   II-159, V-408, N72
proportional font   I-228, T-109
ProtectEntry procedure   V-143
protocol   II-263, T-181
protocol handler   II-264
   table   II-264
   writing your own   II-324, 326
PrPicFile procedure   II-160, V-408
PrSetError procedure   II-161, V-408
prStl subrecord, of print record   N72
PrStlDialog function   II-158, V-408
PrStlInit function   N95
PrValidate function   II-158, V-408, N72
PScrapStuff data type   I-457
PSetSelfSend function   V-516
Pt2Rect procedure   I-175
PtInRect function   I-175
PtInRgn function   I-185
Ptr data type   I-78
PtrAndHand function   II-376
PtrToHand function   II-375
PtrToXHand function   II-375
PtrZone function   II-38
PtToAngle procedure   I-175
pulse-width encoding   T-224
purge bit   II-25
purge warning procedure   II-23
purgeable block   I-76, II-10, 41, T-147
purgeable resource   T-73
PurgeMem procedure   II-40, N51
PurgeSpace procedure   IV-78
purging   T-148
purging a block   I-76, II-14, 40
PutScrap function   I-459

Q

quadrature encoding   T-234
quadrature signal   T-234
QDError function   V-145
QDProcs data type   I-197
QDProcsPtr data type   I-197
QElem data type   II-373
QElemPtr data type   II-373
QHdr data type   II-372

QHdrPtr data type II-373
QTypes data type II-373
queue II-373, N2
  drive II-127, IV-181
  driver I/O II-180, 191
  file I/O II-97, 124, IV-115, 175
  manipulation II-382
  Time Manager IV-299
  vertical retrace II-350, 352
  volume-control-block II-125, IV-176
QuickDraw I-11, 135, IV-23, N21, P-60, 77,
    T-19, 51, 57, 63, 66, 82, 102, 104, 105,
    107, 114, 119, 124, 142, 143, 215, 216,
    238
  See also Color QuickDraw
  color N120, N163
  communication with Font Manager I-224,
    IV-33
  cursors and P-84
  fonts and P-82
  graphics T-83
  icons and P-83
  internal pict def N21
  lines and P-78
  patterns and P-81
  pens and P-78
  picture P-86
  polygons and P-87
  programming model P-63
  regions and P-85
  routines I-162, IV-23
  shapes and P-79
  text and I-233
  text measuring N26
  using I-160
Quit command I-57

R

radio button I-312, 404, T-54
  dimmed T-55
Radius FPD N100
RAM III-17, IV-246, T-2, 140, 211
  accessing from cards C13-11
  Macintosh SE C12-5
  Macintosh II C1-5
RAM Serial Driver I-13, II-246, T-169
  advanced Control calls II-254
  Device Manager calls II-248

routines II-249
RAMBase global variable I-87
RAMSDClose procedure II-250
RAMSDOpen function II-249
Random function I-194
random number generator I-194, II-407
randSeed global variable I-163, 194
raster scanning T-214
raw key codes V-190
'RDEV' resource IV-216
rDocProc P-92
Read function
  high-level IV-109
    Device Manager II-178
    File Manager II-92
  low-level IV-139
    Device Manager II-185
    File Manager II-110
read-modify-write indivisible bus operation C5-8
read transactions C3-6
read/write permission II-83, IV-95
ReadDateTime function II-378
reading from files P-131
ReadPacket function II-327
ReadRest function II-327
RealColor function V-141
RealFont function I-223
reallocating a block I-76, II-14
ReallocHandle procedure II-35
real-time clock T-222
RecoverHandle function II-35, N23
Rect data type I-141
rectangle I-140, P-77, 80
  routines I-174
RectInRgn function I-185
RectRgn procedure I-183
REdit T-79
reference number of a resource file I-105
reference value
  control I-316
  window I-274
region I-141, T-86
  grafPort T-92
  QuickDraw and P-85
  routines I-181
  of a window P-92
Region data type I-141
register 0 V-365
register 3 V-365
register-based routines I-90, 93
register-saving conventions I-94
RegisterName function II-322, V-513

relative handle II-24
release timer II-270
released, defined C2-8
ReleaseResource procedure I-120, P-103, 179
releasing blocks P-51
relocatable block I-75, II-10, P-47, T-147
    allocating II-32
    releasing II-33
    properties of IV-78
RelRspCB function II-319, V-514
RelString function IV-234
RelTCB function II-319, V-513
RemoveName function II-324, V-513
removing
    controls P-112
    menus P-101
Rename function
    high-level II-96, IV-114
    low-level II-118, IV-153
reply record P-125
    structure of P-127
ReqListRec record V-144
ResEdit N40, P-140, T-79
    resource editor T-80
reselection phase IV-286
ResErr global variable I-116
ResError function I-116
ResErrProc global variable I-116, N78
reserved bits N117, P-163
Reserved field C8-7
reserved heap space P-58
ReserveEntry procedure V-143
/RESET C2-5, C3-2, C6-2, C13-9
reset signal C3-2
ResetAlrtStage procedure I-423
ResLoad global variable I-118, N50
resource I-103, P-19, T-15, 19, 34, 66, 68, 154
    access T-72
    attributes I-111, T-73
        getting I-121
        setting I-122
    data I-106, T-69, 72
    file I-105, T-44, 57, 69, 70, 74
        attributes I-126
        current I-105, 116
        fonts in I-234
        format I-128
        information I-121
        opening and closing I-114
        opening order I-104
        structure I-105
    fork I-105, II-81, IV-93, N74, P-122, T-68

getting and disposing of I-118
graphic I-147
header I-128
ID I-108, T-69, 76
    of fonts I-234
    of owned resources I-109
locking C5-7
map I-106, 113, P-20, T-69, 72
name I-110
owned I-109
reference I-110, T-73
    format I-130
specification I-103, 107
templates I-108, 423
type I-103, T-69, 75
    determining I-117
    list I-107, IV-17, V-30
    reserved N32
within a resource I-127
resource compiler P-140
resource decompiler P-140
resource editor P-140, T-79
Resource Manager I-9, 101, IV-15, V-29, N78,
    N116, P-20, T-19, 49, 57, 68, 72, 103,
    151, 154
    routines I-113, IV-15
    using I-112
resources, and dialogs I-402, 423
resources, Finder-related III-10
resources, for menus I-363, P-100
resources, max N141
resources, of windows I-272
resources, pointed to by other resources I-127
response BDS II-288, 314
ResrvMem procedure II-39
Restart command V-586
Restart procedure II-385
RestoreA5 procedure II-386, N136
RestoreEntries procedure V-144
ResType data type I-107
result code I-116, II-27, 374, N117
    assembly language I-94
    list III-205, V-597
    Resource Manager IV-18
Resume button T-188
resume procedure I-411, II-358, T-188
ResumeProc global variable I-411
Return From Execution (RTE) instruction T-189
Return key T-56
RetransType data type II-298
retry N9

count II-266
interval II-266
Revert to Saved command I-57
RevisionLevel field C8-7
Rez P-140, T-80
RGB T-99, 100
RGB space V-42, T-100
RGB value V-48, T-101
RGBBackColor procedure V-68
RGBColor record V-48, V-136
RGBForeColor procedure V-68
RGB2CMY procedure V-175
RGB2HSL procedure V-175
RGB2HSV procedure V-175
RGetResource function V-30
RgnHandle data type I-142
RgnPtr data type I-142
RMaker N46
RmveReference N2
RmveResource procedure I-113, 124
RmvTime procedure IV-300
RndSeed global variable I-195
ROM III-18, IV-247, T-2, 14, 213
    declaration C8-2, C9-11
    Macintosh SE C12-6
    Macintosh II C1-5
ROM checksum N139
ROM resource IV-18, V-30
    list IV-19, V-32
    map IV-19
    overriding IV-20
ROM Serial Driver I-13, II-246, IV-225
    advanced Control calls IV-226
    Device Manager calls II-248
    routines II-250
ROM85 N117
ROMBase global variable I-87, II-383, III-18,
    IV-236, C1-5, C12-6
ROMFont0 global variable I-233
ROMMapInsert global variable IV-19
romStart constant C1-5, C12-6
root directory IV-91
routine selector I-483
    File Manager IV-118
    List Manager IV-269
    SCSI Manager IV-289
routing table II-265
Routing Table Maintenance Protocol (RTMP)
    II-265, T-183
row width I-143, T-89
rowBytes N117, P-162
rPage N33, N72

/RQST C2-5, C5-2, 3, 6, 9, C6-2, 8
RS-232C T-229
RS-422 T-228
RsrcMapEntry function IV-16
RsrcZoneInit procedure I-114
RstFilLock function
    high-level II-96, IV-114
    low-level II-117, IV-152
RstFLock function II-96, IV-114
RTMP II-265
    socket II-265
    stub II-265
R/W C13-9

S

safety
    Macintosh SE C14-10
    Macintosh II C7-5
sample program I-13, P-139, 156
sampled sound synthesizer V-475, T-173
sampling edge, defined C2-8
SANE II-405, IV-69, *See also* C SANE
    Library
Save As command I-57, T-157
Save command I-57, T-157
SaveEntries procedure V-144
SaveOld procedure I-296
SaveUpdate global variable I-297
SaveVisRgn global variable I-293
sBlock data type C8-2, C8-3
sBootRecord V-422
SCalcSPtr function V-455
SCalcStep function V-453
ScalePt procedure I-195
scaling factors I-218
SCardChanged function V-452
SCC III-22, IV-248, N2, N56
    interrupts II-198
SCCRd global variable II-199, III-25
SCCWr global variable II-199, III-25
schematic
    NuBus Test Card CFoldout 3
    SCSI-NuBus Test Card C10-14
SCkCardStatus function V-450
SCNoInc N96
scrap
    between applications I-453

in TextEdit I-373, 388
scrap file I-453, T-63
Scrap Manager I-12, 451, IV-61, T-20, 63
   routines I-457
ScrapCount global variable I-457
ScrapHandle global variable I-457
ScrapName global variable I-457
ScrapSize global variable I-457
ScrapState global variable I-457
ScrapStuff data type I-457
Scratch8 global variable I-85
Scratch20 global variable I-85
ScrDmpEnb global variable I-258
screen
   buffer III-18, 19, IV-247, T-82, 142, 215
   configuration V-127
   font T-118
   location P-161
   size P-161
   width P-162
screen utility resource T-78
screenBits global variable I-145, 163, N2,
   N117
screenBits.baseAddr N117, P-161
screenBits.bounds N117, P-161
screenBits.bounds.right P-162
screenBits.rowBytes N117, P-162
ScreenRes procedure I-473
screenRow N117
ScrHRes global variable I-473
script V-294, T-19, 82, 110
Script Interface System V-295, T-111
Script Manager V-9, V-293, T-19, 110
   features V-303
   Print Action routine N174
routines V-306
scripts (HyperTalk) P-150
ScriptUtil macro V-306
'scrn' resource V-127, P-88
ScrnBase global variable II-19, 21, N117, T-
   143
scroll bar I-47, 312, T-20, 34, 48, 53, 54
   updating I-291
scrolling arrow T-46
scrolling menu indicator T-46
ScrollRect procedure I-187
ScrpSTElement V-266
ScrpSTTable array V-266
ScrVRes global variable I-473
SCSI *See* Small Computer Standard Interface
SCSI driver N159
SCSI Manager IV-283, V-573, N96

routines IV-289, V-574
   writing a driver IV-292
SCSI-NuBus Test Card C10-10. *See also* cards
   (NuBus); Macintosh II; NuBus; NuBus Test
   Card
   hardware overview C10-11
   PAL descriptions C10-15
   PAL listings for CB-1
   schematic of C10-12
   software overview C10-10
   timing diagram C10-14
SCSICmd function IV-290, N96
SCSIComplete function IV-291, N96
SCSIDispatch trap macro V-574
SCSIGet function IV-289, N96
SCSIInstr data type IV-287
SCSIMsgIn function V-575
SCSIMsgOut function V-575
SCSIRBlind function IV-290, V-574, 576, N96
SCSIRead function IV-290, N96
SCSIReset function IV-289
SCSISelANfunction V-575
SCSISelect function IV-290
SCSIStat function IV-291, N96
SCSIWBlind function IV-291, V-574, 576
SCSIWrite function IV-291
SCStop N96
SDeleteSRTRec function V-451
sDriver directory C8-13, 14
sDriver record C9-5
SdVolume global variable II-232
SE-Bus expansion interface 12-6, 13-5 *See
   also* cards (Macintosh SE); Macintosh SE
SearchProc function V-146
Seawell Inspector P-151
SEBlock packed record V-441
second sound buffer N113
second video buffer N113
secondary ordering V-291
Secs2Date procedure II-380
sector II-211, T-163
SectRect function I-175
SectRgn procedure I-184
SeedCFill procedure V-71
SeedFill procedure IV-24
segment II-55, T-150
Segment Loader I-12, II-53, IV-83, P-53, T-21,
   135, 147, 150
   error T-190
   routines II-57
selecting IV-5
selection phase IV-286, T-175

selection range I-375
SelectWindow procedure I-284, P-37, 98, 179
SelIText procedure I-422, P-110
SendBehind procedure I-286
SendRequest function II-316, V-513
SendReset command V-363, 364
SendResponse function II-317, V-513
sequence number of a datagram II-266
SerClrBrk function II-253
'SERD' resource IV-225
SerGetBuf function II-253
SerHShake function II-251, N56
serial communication II-245, T-176, 246
  hardware III-22
Serial Communications Controller (SCC) III-
      22, IV-248, C1-3, C12-4, T-177, 180,
      181, 192, 216, 217, 228
serial data II-245, T-177
Serial Driver I-13, II-243, IV-225, T-22, 169,
      176, 229
  advanced Control calls II-254, IV-226
  Device Manager calls II-248
  routines II-249
serial I/O T-228
serial port IV-225, T-131
SerReset function II-250
SerSetBrk function II-252
SerSetBuf function II-251
SerShk data type II-252
SerStaRec data type II-253
SerStatus function II-253, N56
server V-522
Service Request Enable V-366
session V-522
SetADBInfo function V-370
SetAppBase procedure II-28
SetApplBase procedure II-28
SetApplLimit procedure II-30
SetCatInfo function IV-156
SetCCursor procedure V-75, P-88, 179
SetChooserAlert function V-431
SetClientID procedure V-147
SetClikLoop procedure I-390
SetClip procedure I-166
SetCPixel procedure V-70
SetCRefCon procedure I-327
SetCTitle procedure I-321
SetCtlAction procedure I-328
SetCtlColor procedure V-222
SetCtlMax procedure I-327
SetCtlMin procedure I-326
SetCtlValue procedure I-326

SetCursor procedure I-167, P-84, 179
SetDAFont procedure I-412
SetDateTime function II-379
SetDefaultStartup procedure V-354
SetDeskCPat procedure V-210
SetDeviceAttribute procedure V-124
SetDItem procedure I-421, N34
SetEmptyRgn procedure I-183
SetEntries procedure V-143
SetEntryColor procedure V-165
SetEntryUsage procedure V-165
SetEnvirons function V-314
SetEOF function P-132, 180
  high-level II-93, IV-111
  low-level II-112, IV-142
SetEventMask procedure II-70
SetFileInfo function
  high-level II-95, IV-114
  low-level II-116, IV-150
SetFilLock function
  high-level II-95, IV-114
  low-level II-116, IV-151
SetFilType function II-117, IV-153
SetFInfo function II-95, IV-114
SetFLock function II-95, IV-114
SetFontLock procedure I-223
SetFPos function P-131, 132, 180
  high-level II-93, IV-110
  low-level II-111, IV-141
SetFractEnable IV-32
  routine V-180
SetFScaleDisable procedure IV-32
SetGDevice procedure V-123
SetGrowZone procedure II-42
SetHandleSize procedure II-34
SetItem procedure I-357, P-104, 180
SetItemCmd procedure V-240
SetItemIcon procedure I-359, V-246
SetItemMark procedure I-359, V-246
SetItemStyle procedure I-360
SetIText procedure I-422
SetItmIcon procedure I-359
SetItmMark procedure I-359
SetItmStyle procedure I-360
SetMaxCtl procedure I-327
SetMCEntries procedure V-239
SetMCInfo procedure V-239
SetMenuBar procedure I-355, P-102, 180
SetMenuFlash procedure I-361
SetMFlash procedure I-361
SetMinCtl procedure I-326
SetOrigin procedure I-166, N72, P-76, 180

SetOSDefault procedure V-355
SetPalette procedure V-162
SetPBits procedure I-165
SetPenState procedure I-169, P-180
SetPort procedure I-165, P-63, 64, 67, 87, 97, 180
SetPortBits procedure I-165
SetPortPix procedure V-76
SetPt procedure I-193
SetPtrSize procedure II-37
SetRecRgn macro I-183
SetRect procedure I-174
SetRectRgn procedure I-183
SetResAttrs procedure I-122, N78
SetResFileAttrs procedure I-127
SetResInfo procedure I-122
SetResLoad procedure I-118, N50
SetResPurge procedure I-126, N111
SetRsl N128
SetScript function V-313
SetSelfSend function V-514
SetSoundVol procedure II-233
SetStdCProcs procedure V-77
SetStdProcs procedure I-198
SetString procedure I-468
SetStylHandle procedure V-268
SetSysJust procedure V-316
SetTagBuffer function II-214
SetTime procedure II-380
SetTimeout procedure V-356
SetTrapAddress procedure II-384, IV-234, N2
setting up menus P-101
SetUpA5 procedure II-386, N136
SetVideoDefault procedure V-355
SetVol function
    high-level II-89, IV-107
    low-level II-105, IV-132
SetWinColor procedure V-207
SetWindowPic procedure I-293
SetWordBreak procedure I-390
SetWRefCon procedure I-293
SetWTitle procedure I-284
SetZone procedure II-31, N8
SEvtEnb global variable I-443
SExec Block V-441, C8-2, 3
SExec function V-452
SFGetFile procedure I-523, N47, N77, N80, P-125, 162, 181
SFindDevBase function V-451
SFindsInfoRecPtr function V-455
SFindsRsrcPtr function V-456
SFindStruct function V-446

SFPGetFile procedure I-526
SFPPutFile procedure I-523
SFPutFile procedure I-519, P-125, 128, 162, 181
SFReply data type I-519
SFSaveDisk global variable I-519, IV-72, N80
SFTypeList data type I-523
SGetBlock function V-445
SGetCString function V-445
SGetDriver function V-455
shapes, QuickDraw and P-79
shared bit N116
shared files V-xxx, N116
Shell *See* MPW Shell
shell application T-124
shell script T-242
ShieldCursor procedure I-474
Shift key P-34, T-40, 43, 47, 62
ShowControl procedure I-322, P-113, 114, 181
ShowCursor procedure I-168, P-84, 181
ShowDItem procedure IV-59
ShowHide procedure I-285
ShowPen procedure I-168
ShowWindow procedure I-285
Shut Down command V-586
Shutdown Manager V-585, T-23
    routines V-587
    trap macro V-587
ShutDwnInstall procedure V-588
ShutDwnPower procedure V-587
ShutDwnRemove procedure V-588
ShutDwnStart procedure V-587
signal line determinacy C3-3
Signals procedure N88
signature III-9, T-126
SignedByte data type I-78
SIMM *See* Single In-Line Memory Module
sine wave T-171
SInfoRecord packed record V-447
single data cycle transactions C3-6
Single In-Line Memory Module (SIMM) IV-246, N176, T-212
SIntInstall function V-427, C9-9
SIntRemove function V-427, C9-9
65C23 Versatile Interface Adapter (VIA1 and VIA2) C1-3
Size data type II-18
size
    of screen P-161
    of parameters I-90
    of variables I-85
size box I-287 *See also* grow region

size correction II-24
SizeControl procedure I-326, P-113, 181
SizeResource function I-121
SizeRsrc function I-121
SizeWindow procedure I-290, P-98, 181
slave, defined C2-8
SlopeFromAngle function I-475
slot C3-3
   defined C2-9
slot allocations C4-6
slot device interrupts C9-8
slot ID
   defined C2-9
   signals C2-5
slot interrupts V-426
Slot Manager V-435, T-22, 209, C8-2
   routines V-437
Slot Parameter Block V-439
Slot Resource Table V-437
slot space C3-3, C4-2
   defined C2-9
SlotVInstall function V-567
SlotVRemove function V-567
Small Computer Standard Interface (SCSI) IV-251, 285, T-3, 163, 175, 217, 227
   driver N159
   Manager T-22, 175
   pseudo DMA N96
   Status phase N96
SmallFract2Fix function V-175
Smalltalk P-147
'snd ' resource V-476, 490
SndAddModifier function V-478
SndChannel record V-477, 481
SndCommand packed record V-483
SndControl function V-479
SndDisposeChannel function V-479
SndDoCommand function V-479
SndDoImmediate function V-479
SndNewChannel function V-477
SndPlay function V-477
SNextsRsrc function V-443
SNextTypesRsrc function V-443
'snth' resource V-476, 495
socket II-265, IV-229, T-181
   client II-265, T-181
   listener II-265
      writing your own II-324, 329
   number II-265
   table II-265
SOffsetData function V-452

software architecture of the Macintosh P-12
      See also applications;
         programs/programming
software overrun error II-246, T-178
SONY driver N70
Sony Sound Chip T-224
sorting, int'l N153
sound V-19
   without clicking N19
Sound cdev V-325
sound buffer II-233, III-18, 21, IV-247, N2, N9, T-142, 188
Sound Driver I-13, II-221, T-22, 169, 170
   hardware II-233
   routines II-231
sound generator II-223, III-20, IV-247, T-142, 223
Sound Manager V-473, T-22, 169, 172
   commands V-482, 486
   routines V-477
   synthesizers T-173
sound procedure I-409, 411, 425
sound synthesizer T-170
SoundBase global variable III-21
SoundDone function II-232
SoundLevel global variable II-234
SoundPtr global variable II-227
source files P-139
source transfer mode I-157
/SP C2-5, C3-5, C6-2
space state II-246
SpaceExtra procedure I-172, P-82, 182
SPAlarm global variable *See* parameter RAM
SPATalkA global variable *See* parameter RAM
SPATalkB global variable *See* parameter RAM
SpBlock packed record V-439
SPClikCaret global variable *See* parameter RAM
SPConfig global variable II-305
speaker volume II-232, 371, T-132
SPFont global variable *See* parameter RAM
SPKbd global variable *See* parameter RAM
split bar I-49
SPMisc2 global variable *See* parameter RAM
spool printing II-151, 153, T-116
spool-a-page N72
SPortSel data type II-249
SPPortA global variable *See* parameter RAM
SPPortB global variable *See* parameter RAM
SPPrint global variable *See* parameter RAM
sPRAMInit record structure C8-18

SPRAMRecord packed record V-448,
SPrimaryInit function V-452
SProcRec record V-146
SPtrToSlot function V-451
spurious attempt T-189
SPutPRAMRec function V-449
/SPV C2-5, C3-5, C6-2
SPValid global variable *See* parameter RAM
SPVolCtl global variable *See* parameter RAM
square wave T-171
square-wave sound T-224
square-wave synthesizer II-223, 225, T-170
SReadByte function V-444
SReadDrvrName function V-444
SReadFHeader function V-449
SReadInfo function V-446
SReadLong function V-445
SReadPBSize function V-453
SReadPRAMRec function V-448
SReadStruct function V-446
SReadWord function V-445
sResource V-437, C8-3
    directory V-437, C8-4, 9
    list V-437
    list entries C8-4, 10, 12
    type format C8-12
sRsrc_BootRec C8-14
sRsrc_DrvrDir C8-13
sRsrcFlags C8-16
sRsrcHWDevId C8-16
SRsrcInfo function V-442
sRsrc_Icon C8-13
sRsrc_LoadRec C8-14
sRsrc_Name C8-13
sRsrc_Type C8-12
SSearchSRT function V-454
stack I-73, II-17, C12-5, P-46, T-142, 144
stack frame I-96, II-17, T-145
stack overflow error T-190
stack-based routines I-90
StackSpace function IV-78
StageList data type I-424
stages of an alert I-409
Standard Apple Numeric Environment (SANE)
    T-184, 207 *See also* C SANE Library
Standard C Library P-140, 141
Standard File Package I-12, 515, IV-71, N2,
    N44, N47, N80, P-123, 125, T-14, 21, 77,
    154, 157
    dialog box T-157
    routines I-519

/START C1-8, C2-5, C3-4, C5-2, 6, 7,
    C6-2, 8
start bit II-245, T-177
start cycle, defined C2-9
Start Manager V-347, T-23
    routines V-352
StartSound procedure II-231, N19
startup V-349
    installing a driver at C9-5
startup applications P-21, T-124
startup screen V-121
Startup device cdev V-325
startup process V-422
Stash function II-195
stationery pads N115
Status function
    high-level II-179
    low-level II-186
status information II-176, C3-9
status monitoring, in graphics port record P-74
status phase IV-286, T-176
status routine of a driver II-187, 194
status routines C9-17
StdArc procedure I-199
StdBits procedure I-199
StdComment procedure I-199
StdGetPic procedure I-200
StdLine procedure I-198
StdOval procedure I-199
StdPoly procedure I-199
StdPutPic procedure I-200
StdRect procedure I-198
StdRgn procedure I-199
StdRRect procedure I-198
StdText procedure I-198
StdTxMeas function I-199
STElement record V-262
StillDown function I-259
stop alert P-106, 107, T-59
stop bit II-245, T-177
StopAlert function I-419, V-284, P-109, 182
StopSound procedure II-232
STR N29
string comparison I-501, 506, II-376, N178
string list I-468
    resource format I-476
string manipulation I-468
StringHandle data type I-78
StringPtr data type I-78
StringToNum procedure I-490
StringWidth function I-173, N26
StripAddress function V-593

Str32 data type II-298
Str255 data type I-78
structure region of a window I-271, P-92, T-51
StScrpRec V-265
StuffHex procedure I-195, P-81
style *See* character style
Style data type I-152
style dialog II-149
Style menu I-61
style record P-118
StyleItem data type I-152
StyleRun V-261
subclass/subclassing P-147
subdirectory IV-89, T-155
Sublaunching N126
submenus *See* menus/menu items
submenu delay V-24
SubPt procedure I-193
SUpdateSRT function V-454
superclass P-147
super slot C3-3
super slot space C3-3, C4-2
    defined C2-9
SwapMMUMode procedure V-593, C1-6
Switcher N2, T-27, 135
switch-launching T-123
SWSynthPtr data type II-225
SWSynthRec data type II-225
synchronous execution
    AppleTalk Manager II-273
    Device Manager II-180
    File Manager II-97, IV-115
synchronous modem T-229
SynListHandle global variable V-182
synthesizer buffer II-225, T-172
synthesizers V-475
synthetic font V-182
SysBeep procedure II-385, V-592
SysEdit function I-441
SysEnvirons function V-5, N129, N156
SysEnvRec record V-6
SysError procedure II-362, V-572
SysEvtMask global variable II-70
SysFontFam global variable IV-31
SysFontSiz global variable IV-31
SysMap global variable I-114
SysMapHndl global variable I-114
SysParam global variable II-369
SysParmType data type II-370
SysPPtr data type II-370
SysResName global variable I-114

System
    clock (NuBus) C2-6
    environment record V-6
    error alert II-357, T-187
        table II-357, 359, T-188
    error ID II-357, T-187
    error recovery T-188
    event mask I-254, II-70
    font I-219, IV-31
        size I-219, IV-31
    globals P-161
    heap I-74, II-9, N83, P-46, 164
        size N83, N113
    out-of-memory conditions and P-57
    startup
        environment IV-256
        information II-120, IV-160, 164
    traps III-215, IV-305, V-603
    use of memory by P-52
    versions IV-xi
        3.2 N96
    window I-270, 438
System Error Handler I-13, II-18, 355, IV-231,
        V-571, T-23, 142, 146, 186, 187
    routine II-362
system event T-39
System file I-103, IV-255, V-34, P-20, T-2, 16,
        26, 38, 59, 77, 122, 157
System Folder T-122, 131, 133, 134
system font T-106
system heap T-141
system heap zone T-145
system resource T-71, 77
system shutdown T-184
system software T-26, 122
system startup T-184
    alert messages T-190
system startup disk T-132, 133
system startup information T-40, 160
System V Interface Definition T-239, 245
SystemClick procedure I-441, P-35, 182
SystemEdit function I-441
SystemEvent function I-442, N5, N85
SystemMenu procedure I-443
SystemTask procedure I-442, 444, II-189, N85
SystemZone function II-32
SysZone global variable II-19, 21, 32, N2

T

Tab key T-157
tag byte II-24, IV-223
tags N94
Talk command V-363, 364
target device IV-285, T-175
TBox P-143
TDftBitsBlk record V-414
TEActivate procedure I-385
TEAutoView procedure IV-57
TECalText procedure I-390
teCarHook N82
Technical Introduction to the Macintosh Family
    P-xviii
TEClick procedure I-384, P-118, 182
TECopy procedure I-386, P-119, 182
TECut procedure I-385, P-119, 182
TEDeactivate procedure I-385
TEDelete procedure I-387, P-119, 182
TEDispatch V-267
TEDispose procedure I-383, P-118, 183
TEDoText global variable I-391, N82
TEFromScrap function I-389
TEGetHeight function V-269, N131
TEGetOffset function V-268
TEGetPoint function V-269
TEGetScrapLen function I-389
TEGetStyle procedure V-269
TEGetText function I-384
TEHandle data type I-374
teHiHook N82
TEIdle procedure I-384
TEInit procedure I-383, P-107, 118, 183
TEInsert procedure I-387, P-120, 183
TEKey procedure I-385, P-119, 183
telnet T-247
templates P-9, T-76
TENew function I-383, P-118, 183
tenure, defined C2-9
TEPaste procedure I-386, P-119, 183
TEPinScroll procedure IV-57
TEPtr data type I-374
TERec data type I-377
TERecal global variable I-391
TEReplaceStyle procedure V-270
TEScrapHandle function I-389
TEScroll procedure I-388, N22, N131, P-120
TEScrpHandle global variable I-389
TEScrpLength global variable I-389, N82
TESelView procedure IV-57

TESetJust procedure I-387
teSelRect N82
TESetScrapLen procedure I-390
TESetSelect procedure I-385, N127
TESetStyle procedure V-269, N131
TESetText procedure I-383, N18
test cards *See* NuBus Test Card; SCSI-NuBus
    Test Card
TestControl function I-325
TestDeviceAttribute function V-124
testing V-28
TestPattern field C8-7
TEStyleRec V-261
TEStyleTable V-262
TEStylInsert procedure V-268, N131
TEStylNew function V-268, N131
TEStylPaste procedure V-269
TEToScrap function I-389
TEUpdate procedure I-387
text
    characteristics I-151
    Color QuickDraw and P-88
    description, in graphics port record P-71
    drawing I-233, V-81
    in a dialog/alert I-404, 408, P-110
    mask mode V-83
    selection I-375
    streaming II-165
'TEXT' data type I-455
text editing T-60
text justification T-112
TextBox procedure I-388, P-115, 183
TextEdit I-12, 371, IV-57, V-259, N82, N127,
    N131, N156, P-115, T-20, 58, 60, 110,
    112
    routines I-383, IV-57, V-267
    scrap I-373, 388
TextFace procedure I-171, P-82, 184
TextFont procedure I-171, P-82, 184
TextMode procedure I-171, P-82, 184
TextSize procedure I-171, P-82, 184
TextStyle V-265
TextWidth function I-173, N131
TFSTagData IV-223
TGetRotnBlk record V-415
TGetRslBlk record V-412, N173
TGnlData record V-410
theGDevice V-118
TheMenu global variable I-357, V-244
thePort global variable I-162, 165, N25
TheZone global variable II-31
32-bit to 24-bit address translations C4-4

thought police N117
thousands separator I-497
THPrint data type II-149
thread record IV-173
three-state, defined C2-10
thumb I-312
THz data type II-22
TickCount function I-260
ticks I-246, P-164, T-43
Ticks global variable I-260, II-198, N2
Time global variable II-198, 369, 378
Time Manager IV-297, N2, T-23, 185, 186
    routines IV-300
time operations II-377
TimeDBRA variable V-352
timeout C8-18, N9
TimeSCCDB variable V-352
TimeSCSIDB variable V-352
timing
    arbitration C5-5, C6-8
    data transfer C6-7
    of NuBus block read transaction C3-13
    of NuBus block write transaction C3-14
    of NuBus write transaction C3-8
    for reading and writing RAM from a card C13-14
    requirements C6-7
    summary C6-8
    transaction C5-5
    utility C6-7
    of video and MC68000 access to RAM C13-12
timing-sensitive code P-163
/TM0, /TM1 C2-5, C3-4, C6-2
TMON N7, P-151
TmpResLoad global variable IV-19
TMTask data type IV-299
TObject P-147
ToExtFS global variable II-128
toggled command I-53, 357
tolerant colors V-155
Tone data type II-225
Tones data type II-225
Toolbox I-9, P-17, 90
    calls P-166
Toolbox Event Manager I-11, 241, V-189, T-19, 28, 36, 47, 50, 52, 229, 231
    routines I-257
Toolbox Utilities I-12, 465, IV-63, T-21
    routines I-467, IV-63
ToolScratch global variable I-85
TopMapHndl global variable I-115

TopMem function II-44
TopMenuItem global variable V-249
TOval P-143
TPPrint data type II-149
TPPrPort data type II-147
TPrDlg N95
TPrInfo data type II-150
TPrint data type II-149
TPrJob data type II-151
TPrPort data type II-147
TPrSt1 data type II-152
TPrStatus data type II-161
TPrXInfo data type II-152
trace exception T-189
track T-163
track cache IV-224, N81
track on a disk II-211
TrackBox function IV-50, N79
TrackControl function I-323, P-114, 184
TrackGoAway function I-288, P-98, 184
transaction II-266
    defined C2-9
    ID II-266
    release II-270
    request II-266
    response II-266
transaction timing C5-5
Transcendental Functions Package I-13, II-403, 407, V-595, T-3, 77
transfer instruction block IV-287
transfer mode I-156, V-57
transfer mode coding C3-5
Transliterate function V-311
Transmission Control Protocol/Internet Protocol (TCP/IP) T-247
trap T-25, 217
TRAP instruction N2
trap dispatch table I-87, IV-13, T-24
    routines II-383
trap dispatcher I-89, T-24
trap macro I-88, 90
    list III-215, IV-305, V-603
trap mechanism T-24
trap number I-89, 384, IV-13
Trap on Overflow (TRAPV) instruction T-189
trap patching N25
trap word I-88, IV-13
TrapType data type IV-233
TRel *See* transaction release
TReq *See* transaction request
TResp *See* transaction response
trigonometric functions II-407

TRslRec record V-411
TRslRg record V-411
try again later C3-10
TSetRslBlk record V-414
24-bit to 32-bit address translations C4-4
type coercion I-79, V-66, V-200
type size *See* font size
txRatio N35

U

/UDS C13-9
UNamAcc N6
unasserted, defined C2-10
Undo command I-59, P-24, T-47
unimplemented core routine T-189
unimplemented instruction I-88, T-25
UnImplTrapNum N156
UnionRect procedure I-175
UnionRgn procedure I-184
UniqueID function I-121
Unique1ID function IV-16
unit attention N92
unit number II-191, IV-215
unit table II-191, IV-215, N71
universal defprocs V-206
UNIX Operating System T-6, 206, 238
UNLK N88
unloading segments P-56
UnloadNBP function II-324
UnloadScrap function I-458
UnloadSeg procedure II-59, P-56, 184
unlocked block I-76, II-10, T-147
unlocking a block I-76, II-41
UnlockRng function IV-139
UnlodeScrap function I-458
unmounted volume II-79, IV-92, P-122, T-158
UnmountVol function
   high-level II-90, IV-108
   low-level II-106, IV-134
UnpackBits procedure I-470, N86
unpurgeable block I-76, II-10, 42, T-147
update event I-244, 278, P-34, T-37, 40, 52
   event message I-252
update region of a window I-272, T-52
   maintenance I-291
UpdateResFile procedure I-125, N116
updating windows P-97
UpdtControl procedure IV-53

UpdtDialog procedure IV-60
uppercase T-76, 158
UprString procedure II-377
use type II-305
User Interface Toolbox I-9, T-7, 14, 18
   components T-17
user bytes II-266
user groups T-257
user interface guidelines I-23, V-13, P-6, 25
UseResFile procedure I-117
userItems N34
   in a dialog I-404, 405
   installing I-421
   routines II-374
USP N2
UTableBase global variable II-192
Utilities, Operating System I-13, II-307, IV-233
   routines II-374, IV-233
Utilities, Toolbox I-12, 465, IV-63
   routines I-467, IV-63
utility signals C2-5, C3-2
utility timing (NuBus card) C6-7

V

valence of a directory IV-91
validity status II-370
ValidRect procedure I-292
ValidRgn procedure I-292
variation code
   control I-328
   window I-298
VBL interrupt *See* vertical blanking interrupt
VBL task II-350, T-185
VBLQueue global variable II-352
VBLTask data type II-350
VCB data type II-125, IV-176
VCB Queue N24, N44
vcbDrvNum N106
VCBQHdr global variable II-126, IV-178
vcbRefNum N106
vector II-196
vector table II-196
VendorInfo C8-19
Vernier procedure N178
Versatile Interface Adapter (VIA) III-39, C1-3, C12-4, T-192, 216, 217, 222

version data   III-10, T-127
version number of a file   II-81, IV-90
version 2 pictures   V-84
vertical blanking interrupt   II-349, III-18, T-185, 214
vertical blanking interval   III-18, T-214
vertical retrace interrupt   I-13, II-349, T-23, 185
Vertical Retrace Manager   I-13, II-347, V-565, T-23, 185
   routines   II-351, V-567
vertical retrace queue   II-350, 352, T-186
VHSelect data type   I-139
VIA   N2
   global variable   I-198, III-39
   interrupts   II-197, III-38, 41
VIABase   N117
video buffer   N2
video card (for Macintosh II)   C11-2. *See also* cards (NuBus); Macintosh II; NuBus
   access to control space for CLUT write   C11-12
   access to RAM space   C11-10
   block diagram   C11-2
   card connectors   C11-18
   color look-up table (CLUT)   C11-11
   declaration ROM operation   C11-15
   firmware levels   C11-17
   Frame Buffer Controller (FBC)   C11-4
   functional operation   C11-2
   horizontal and vertical scan timing   C11-13
   output connector pin assignments   C11-18
   scaled pixel clock periods   C11-5
   scan line horizontal timing regions   C11-6
   scan line vertical timing regions   C11-8
video declaration ROM   C9-11
video device record   C9-12
video display   T-82, 142
Video Driver   C9-10, T-22
   example   C9-18
   routines   C9-13
video interface   III-18, IV-247, T-214
video RAM   C11-9, T-188
video scanning   T-215
view rectangle   I-374, P-116
VInstall function   II-351
virtual key codes   V-190
virtual memory   T-206
virtual paging   T-202
visible
   control   I-316
   window   I-274
visRgn of a grafPort   I-149

/VMA   C13-8
volume (on a disk)   II-79, IV-89, P-133, T-68, 154
   access   T-158
   allocation block map   II-122, IV-162
   attributes   II-121, IV-162
   bitmap   IV-167
   buffer   II-79, IV-92
   control block   II-125, IV-92, 176
   index   II-102
   information   II-121, IV-161, 166
   information block   IV-165
   name   II-79, IV-90
   reference number   II-79, IV-93, 98, P-124
volume allocation block map   T-161
volume bit map   T-161
volume control block   T-161
volume information   T-158, 161
volume name   T-158
volume-control-block queue   II-125, IV-176
volume (speaker)   II-232, 371
/VPA   C13-8
vRefNum   N44, N77
VRemove function   II-351

W

WaitMouseUp function   I-259
WaitNextEvent   N158
Wave data type   II-227
wave table synthesizer   V-475, T-173
waveform   II-223, T-170
   description   II-224, T-172
wavelength   II-223, T-171
WavePtr data type   II-227
'wctb' resource   V-201, 204
WDEF   N110
wDev   N72
WDPBPtr data type   IV-117
WDPBRec data type   IV-127
WDRefNum   N44, N77
white global variable   I-162
width (of screen)   P-162
width tables   N92
WidthListHand global variable   IV-42
WidthPtr global variable   IV-42
WidthTabHandle global variable   IV-42
WidthTable data type   IV-41
WinCTab record   V-202

window I-44, 269, P-91, T-34, 48
 activation I-279
 closing I-45, 283, P-95
 color table V-203
 defining your own I-297
 defproc V-205
 description, in graphics port record P-69
 drawing I-278
 frame I-271, T-51, 52
 list I-274, 277
 mouse and P-97
 mouse event handling in P-36
 opening I-45, 282, P-95
 pointer I-275
 record I-274, 276, P-93
 regions I-271, P-92, T-51
 resources I-272
  format I-302
 sizing I-47, 289
 splitting I-49
 standard state IV-7
 template I-274
 types I-273, P-91
 updating P-97
 user state IV-8
 zooming IV-7, 49
window class I-274, 276
window definition
 function I-272, 298, IV-49, T-49
 ID I-273, 298
Window Manager I-11, 267, IV-49, V-197, P-91, T-20, 29, 36, 37, 48, 57, 76, 95, 97
 port I-271, 282
 routines I-281, IV-50, V-206
 using P-95
window template T-49
WindowList global variable I-255, 277
WindowPeek data type I-275
WindowPtr data type I-275
WindowRecord data type I-276
WMgrCPort V-205
WMgrPort global variable I-282
word I-42, C8-2, T-60
 data type C8-2
 defined C2-10
 in TextEdit I-373
word break routine I-380
word break tables N182
word demarcation T-112
word wraparound I-373, T-60
word-description break tables V-309
word-selection break tables V-309

working directory IV-98, N126
 control block IV-98
 reference number IV-98
workstation V-522
wraparound, of words I-373
Write function
 high-level IV-110
  Device Manager II-179
  File Manager II-92
 low-level IV-140
  Device Manager II-185
  File Manager II-110
write data structure II-306
write transactions 3-Z8530 Serial Communications Controller (SCC) C1-3, C12-4
WriteDDP function II-312, V-513
WriteLAP function II-307, V-513
WriteParam function II-382
WriteResource procedure I-125
writing direction T-112
writing to files P-132
WStateData data type IV-49

X

X2Fix function IV-65
X2Frac function IV-65
XOn/XOff T-178
XorRgn procedure I-185
XPP (Extended Protocol Package) driver V-524, V-527, 530
 access V-533
 example V-531
 result codes V-550
XPP command control block V-549
XPP error reporting V-526
XPP open session commands V-528
XPPParamBlock packed record V-535

Z

zero divide T-189
ZeroScrap function I-458
Zone data type II-22
zone

    AppleTalk Manager II-266
    header II-22
    Memory Manager *See* heap zone
    pointer II-22
    record II-22
    trailer II-22
zoom region T-51
zoom window box IV-8
ZoomWindow procedure IV-50, V-210

INDEX II: CONSTANTS AND FIELD NAMES

A

abbrLen I-500
abOpcode III-50
abResult III-50
abUserReference III-50
accClear I-446
accCopy I-446
accCursor I-446
accCut I-446
accEvent I-446
accMenu I-446
accPaste I-446
accRun I-446, II-189
acCTable V-217
accUndo I-446
acFlags V-217
acNext V-217
acOwner V-217
acRefCon V-217
acReserved V-217
activateEvt I-249
activDev V-331
active I-377
activeFlag I-253
activMask I-254
aCtl II-199
aData II-199
addOver V-61
addPin V-61
addResFailed I-116
addSize V-269
aDefItem I-408
adMax V-61
adMin V-61
aFace IV-41
aFID IV-41
alarm II-370
allocPtr II-22
alphaLock I-253
altDBoxProc I-273
ampCmd V-483
amplitude II-225
amScriptAppFond V-312
app1Evt I-249
app1Mask I-254
app2Evt I-249
app2Mask I-254
app3Evt I-249
app3Mask I-254
app4Evt I-249
app4Mask I-254
appleMark I-219
applFont I-219

appOpen II-58
appPrint II-58
arcProc I-197
aRdCmd II-194
ascent I-173
aSize IV-41
aTalkA II-370
aTalkB II-370
atDrvrVersNum V-6
athens I-219
atp II-313
atpBitMap II-312
atpControl II-312
atpEOMBit II-313
atpHdSz II-312
atpMaxNum II-314
atpRelCode II-313
atpReqCode II-313
atpRespNo II-312
atpRspCode II-313
atpSize II-274
atpSTSBit II-313
atpTransID II-312
atpUserData II-312
atpXOBit II-313
autoKey I-249
autoKeyMask I-254
autoTrack I-329
availableCmd V-482
awCTable V-201
awFlags V-201
awNext V-201
awOwner V-201
aWrCmd II-194
awRefCon V-201
awReserved V-201
axis I-332

B

baseAddr V-52
baud300 II-250
baud600 II-250
baud1200 II-250
baud1800 II-250
baud2400 II-250
baud3600 II-251
baud4800 II-251
baud7200 II-251
baud9600 II-251
baud19200 II-251
baud57600 II-251
bCtl II-199

bData II-199
bdConv I-483, IV-67
bDevCItoh II-152
bDraftLoop II-151
bdsBuffAddr II-314
bdsBuffSz II-314
bdsDataSz II-314
bdsEntrySz II-314
bdsUserData II-314
bFileVers II-151
bitImage I-231
bitsProc I-197
bJDocLoop II-151
bJobX II-151
bkColor I-148, V-50
bkLim II-22
bkPat I-148
bkPixPat V-50
blackColor I-158
blend V-61
blue V-72
blueColor I-158
bold I-227
boldBit I-152
boldItm1 I-424
boldItm2 I-424
boldItm3 I-424
boldItm4 I-424
bounds V-52
boundsRect I-423
boxDrwn1 I-424
boxDrwn2 I-424
boxDrwn3 I-424
boxDrwn4 I-424
breakEvent II-252
brRq II-320
bSpoolLoop II-151
btnState I-253
bufferCmd V-483
buffPtr II-288
buffSize II-288
buttonMsg IV-218
bXtra V-415

C

cairo I-219
calcCRgns I-329
callBack V-481
callBackCmd V-482
cancel I-407
caretHook I-377
caretState I-377

caretTime I-377
cautionIcon I-420
cBodyColor V-220
ccReserved V-218
ccSeed V-218
cdevGenErr V-335
cdevMemErr V-335
cdevResErr V-335
cdevUnset V-335
cellArray IV-264
cells IV-264
cellSize IV-263
century I-498
cFrameColor V-220
charCode I-251
charCodeMask I-250
checkBoxProc I-315
checkMark I-219
chExtra V-50
ciFlags V-159
ciPrivate V-159
ciRGB V-159
ciTolerance V-159
ciUsage V-159
clearDev V-331
clickLoc I-377
clickTime I-377
clikLoc IV-263
clikLoop I-377
clikStuff I-377
clikTime IV-263
clipRgn I-148, V-50
closeDev V-331
cmdInProg V-481
cmdKey I-253
cmpCount V-53
cmpSize V-53
CMY2RGB V-174
cntEmpty II-22
cntHandles II-22
cntNRel II-22
cntRel II-22
code V-482
colrBit I-148, V-50
commandMark I-219
commentProc I-197
config II-370
contRgn I-276, V-199
contrlAction I-317
contrlData I-317
contrlDefProc I-317
contrlHilite I-317
contrlMax I-317
contrlMin I-317
contrlOwner I-317
contrlRect I-317

contrlRFCon I-317
contrlTitle I-317
contrlValue I-317
contrlVis I-317
controlErr II-161
controlList I-276, V-199
copy I-519, 527
copyDev V-331
count II-225, V-482
countShown V-339
courier I-219
crOnly I-377
crossCursor I-474
crsrData V-63
crsrHotSpot V-63
crsrID V-63
crsrlData V-63
crsrMask V-63
crsrType V-63
crsrXData V-63
crsrXHandle V-63
crsrXTable V-63
crsrXValid V-63
cTextColor V-220
ctFlags V-135
cThumbColor V-220
ctSeed V-135
ctsEvent II-252
ctSize V-135
ctTable V-135
currFmt I-497
currLeadingZ I-498
currNegSym I-498
currSym1 I-497
currSym2 I-497
currSym3 I-497
currSymLead I-498
currTrailingZ I-498
cutDev V-331
cyanColor I-158

D

dackRd IV-253
dackWr IV-253
data I-146
data5 II-251
data6 II-251
data7 II-251
data8 II-251
dataBounds IV-264
dataHandle I-276, V-199
dataSize II-288
dateOrder I-497
dateSep I-497
day II-378
dayLdingZ I-498

dayLeading0 I-500
dayOfWeek II-378
days I-500
dBoxProc I-273
dCtlCurTicks II-190
dCtlDelay II-190
dCtlDriver II-190
dCtlEMask II-190
dCtlEnable II-188
dCtlFlags II-190
dCtlMenu II-190
dCtlPosition II-190
dCtlQHdrs II-190
dCtlRefNum II-190
dCtlStorage II-190
dCtlWindows II-190
dDevLaser II-152
ddpCheckSum II-308
ddpDstNet II-308
ddpDstNode II-308
ddpDstSkt II-309
ddpHopCnt II-308
ddpHSzLong II-309
ddpHSzShort II-310
ddpLength II-308, II-310
ddpLenMask II-310
ddpMaxData II-310
ddpSize II-274
ddpSrcNet II-308
ddpSrcNode II-308
ddpSrcSkt II-309
ddpType II-309
deActivDev V-331
decimalPt I-497
denom I-224
descent I-173
deselectMsg IV-218
deskPatID I-281
destRect I-377
device I-148, 224, IV-41
dialogCItem V-201
diamondMark I-219
diBadMount II-396
diFormat II-396
diLoad II-396
diskErrs II-215
diskEvt I-249
diskInPlace II-215
diskMask I-254
dispCntl I-329
diUnload II-396
diVerify II-396
diZero II-396
dlgItems V-339
dlgPtr V-339
dmy I-498

dNeedGoodbye II-188
dNeedLock II-188
dNeedTime II-188
doAll V-269
doBColor V-281
doColor V-269
documentProc I-273
doFace V-269
doFont V-269
doFontName V-281
doMode V-281
doSize V-269
dQDrive II-127, 215
dQDrvSize II-127
dQDrvSz IV-181
dQDrvSz2 IV-181
dQFSID II-127, 215
dQRefNum II-127, 215
dragCntl I-329
drawCntl I-329
dReadEnable II-188
driverEvt I-249
driverMask I-254
drvQType II-373
drvStsCode II-215
dskInit I-483, IV-67
dsNotThe1 V-572
dStatEnable II-188
dtAddr V-466
dtFlags V-466
dtParm V-466
dtReserved V-466
duration II-225
dWritEnable II-188
DYM V-290

E

editField I-408
editOpen I-408
ejectCode II-214
emptyCmd V-482
enableFlags I-345
endMarker V-230
env512KE V-7
env68000 V-7
env68010 V-7
env68020 V-7
envAExtendKbd V-7
envCPUUnknown V-7
environsVersion V-6
envMac V-7
envMacAndPad V-7
envMachUnknown V-7
envMacII V-7
envMacKbd V-7
envMacPlus V-7

envMacPlusKbd V-7
envSE V-7
envStandADBKbd V-7
envUnknownKbd V-7
envXL V-7
equals II-320
errNum I-227
evenParity II-251
every V-482
everyEvent I-254
eveStr I-497
evtNotEnb II-58
evtQMessage II-71
evtQModifiers II-71
evtQWhat II-71
evtQWhen II-71
evtQWhere II-71
evType II-373
extendBit I-152
extra I-227

F

face I-224, IV-41
false32b V-592
family I-224
fdComment IV-105
fdCreator II-84, IV-104
fDesktop II-85, IV-105
fdFlags II-84, IV-104
fdFldr II-84, IV-104
fdIconID IV-105
fDisk II-85, IV-105
fdLocation II-84
FDLocation IV-104
fdPutAway IV-105
fdType II-84, IV-104
fdUnused IV-105
ffAscent IV-36
ffAssoc IV-37
ffDescent IV-36
ffFamID IV-36
ffFirstChar IV-36
ffFlags IV-36
ffIntl IV-37
ffKernOff IV-36
ffKernTab IV-37
ffLastChar IV-36
ffLEading IV-36
ffMode II-225
ffProperty IV-37
fFromUsr II-151
ffStylOff IV-37
ffStyTab IV-37
ffVersion IV-37
ffWidMax IV-36
ffWidthTab IV-37

ffWTabOff IV-36
fgColor I-148, V-50
fHand IV-41
fHasBundle II-85, IV-105
fID IV-41
filler1 I-423
filler2 I-423
fillListMsg IV-217
fillPat I-148
fillPixPat V-50
fImaging II-161
fInvisible II-85, IV-105
firstChar I-231
firstMod V-481
Fix2SmallFract V-174
fixedFont I-232, IV-35
flags II-22, V-481, 482
fLandscape V-415
flPiont IV-67
flPoint I-483
flushCmd V-482
fName I-519, 527, II-58
fOnDesk IV-105
font II-370
fontAscent I-377
fontHandle I-227
fontType I-231
fontWid IV-35
fPgDirty II-161
framingErr II-252
frComment IV-106
fRectHeight I-231
fRectWidth I-231
freeCmd V-482
freqCmd V-483
frFlags IV-105
frLocation IV-105
frOpenChain IV-106
frPutAway IV-106
frRect IV-105
frScroll IV-106
frUnused IV-106
frView IV-105
fsAtMark II-93
fsCurPerm II-100
FSFCBLen IV-97
fsFromLEOF II-93
fsFromMark II-93
fsFromStart II-93
fSize IV-41
fsQType II-373
fsRdPerm II-100
fsRdWrPerm II-100
fsRdWrSHPerm IV-120
fsWrPerm II-100
ftMode II-225

fTrash II-85, IV-105
fType I-519, I-527
fxdFntH IV-35
fxdFntHW IV-35
fxdFntW IV-35

G

gdCCBytes V-119
gdCCDepth V-119
gdCCXData V-119
gdCCXMask V-119
gdCompProc V-119
gdFlags V-119
gdID V-119
gdITable V-119
gdMode V-119
gdNextGD V-119
gdPMap V-119
gdRect V-119
gdRefCon V-119
gdRefNum V-119
gdReserved V-119
gdResPref V-119
gdSearchProc V-119
gdType V-119
geneva I-219
getCancel I-526
GetColor V-174
getDlgID I-525
getDrive I-526
getEject I-526
getNmList I-526
getOpen I-526
getPicProc I-197
getScroll I-526
getSelMsg IV-217
goAwayFlag I-276, 423,
          V-199
good I-519, 527
goodBye II-189
gPort II-147
grafProcs I-148
grafVars V-50
green V-72
greenColor I-158
gzProc II-22

H

hasColorQD V-6
hasFPU V-6
hAxisOnly I-295, I-325
heapData II-22
helvetica I-219
hFactor IV-41
hFstFree II-22

highHook I-377
hilite V-62
hilited I-276
hitDev V-331
hMenu V-230
hotSpot I-146
hour II-378
hOutput IV-41
howOftenCmd V-482
hPic II-161
hPrint II-161
hPrint V-414
hRes V-53
hScroll IV-263
HSL2RGB V-174
hState V-482
HSV2RGB V-174
hText I-377
hwOverrunErr II-252

I

iBandH II-152
iBandV II-152
iBeamCursor I-474
iconBMap V-65
iconData V-65
iconMask V-65
iconMaskData V-65
iconPMap V-65
iCopies II-151
iCurBand II-161
iCurCopy II-161
iCurPage II-161
iDev II-149
iDevBytes II-152
iError V-410
iFileVol II-151
iFstPage II-151
iHandled V-339
iHideCounts V-339
iHRes II-149
iIgnored V-339
iIOAbort II-161
iLstPage II-151
iMax V-411
iMemFullErr II-161
iMin V-411
inButton I-316
inCheckBox I-316
inContent I-287
inDenom IV-41
indent IV-263
inDesk I-287
inDownButton I-316
inDrag I-287
inGoAway I-287

inGrow I-287
initChan0 V-486
initChan1 V-486
initChan2 V-486
initChan3 V-486
initChanLeft V-486
initChanRight V-486
initCmd V-482
initCntl I-329
initDev V-331
initMono V-486
InitPRAMRecs V-438
InitSDeclMgr V-438
initSRate22k V-486
initSRate44k V-486
InitsRsrcTable V-438
initStereo V-486
inMenuBar I-287
inNumer IV-41
inPageDown I-316
inPageUp I-316
inPort I-377
installed II-215
inSysWindow I-287
int10Vers I-497
inThumb I-316
intl1Vers I-500
intUtil I-483
intUtil IV-67
inUpButton I-316
inVBL II-350
inZoomIN IV-49
inZoomOut IV-49
ioCmdAddr II-98
ioCompletion II-98
ioNamePtr II-98
iOpCode V-410
ioQType II-373
ioResult II-98
ioTrap II-98
ioVRefNum II-98
iPFMaxPgs II-152
iPrAbort II-161
iPrBitsCtl II-163, V-409
iPrDevCtl II-163, V-410
iPrDrvrRef II-162
iPrEvtCtl V-410
iPrIOCtl II-163, V-409
iPrSavPFil II-161
iPrVersion II-149
iRgtype V-412
iRowBits II-152
iRslRecCnt V-412
iShowCounts V-339
iTabRes V-139
iTabSeed V-139

italic I-227
italicBit I-152
items I-408
itemsID I-423, 424
iTitle V-339
iTitleHandled V-339
iTitleIgnored V-339
iTotBands II-161
iTotCopies II-161
iTotPages II-161
iTTable V-139
iuDatePString I-504
iuDateString I-504
iuGetInt1 I-504
iuMagIDString I-504
iuMagString I-504
iuMetric I-504
iuSetInt1 I-504
iuTimePString I-504
iuTimeString I-504
iVersion V-339
iVRes II-149
iXRsl V-411, 414
iYRsl V-411, 414

J, K

just I-377
kbdPrint II-370
kernMax I-231
keyBoardtype V-6
keyCodeMask I-250
keyDown I-249
keyDownMask I-254
keyEvtDev V-331
keyUp I-249
keyUpMask I-254
killCode II-194

L

lActivate IV-269
lActive IV-263
lAddColumn IV-269
lAddRow IV-269
lAddToCell IV-269
lapDstAdr II-306
lapHdSz II-306
lapSize II-274
lapSrcAdr II-306
lapType II-306
lastChar I-231
lastClick IV-263
lastHMenu V-228
lastMenu V-228
lastRight V-228
lClikLoop IV-263

lCloseMsg IV-277
lDelColumn IV-270
lDelRow IV-270
lDispose IV-270
lDoDraw IV-270
lDoHAutoScroll IV-265
lDoVautoScroll IV-265
lDraw IV-270
lDrawMsg IV-277
leading I-173
lExtendDrag IV-267
lFind IV-270
lGetCell IV-270
lGetSelect IV-270
lhAscent V-261
lhHeight V-261
lHiliteMsg IV-277
lHiPaintBits V-409
lHiScreenBits V-409
lhTAb V-261
limitRect I-332
lineHeight I-377
lineProc I-197
lineStarts I-377
lInitMsg IV-277
listDefProc IV-263
listFlags IV-263
listMgr IV-67
listSep I-497
lkUp II-320
lkUpReply II-320
lLastClick IV-270
lngDateFmt I-500
lNoDisjoint IV-267
lNoExtend IV-267
lNoNilHilite IV-267
lNoRect IV-267
localRtn I-500
locTable I-231
london I-219
longDay V-290
longDDP II-306
longMonth V-290
longWeek V-290
longYear V-290
lOnlyOne IV-267
losAngeles I-219
lPaintBits II-164
lPaintBits V-409
lPrDocClose V-410
lPrDocOpen V-410
lPrEvtAll V-410
lPrEvtTop V-410
lPrLFSixth II-163
lPrLFStd V-410
lPrLineFeed II-163, V-410

lPrPageClose V-410
lPrPageEnd II-163, V-410
lPrPageOpen V-410
lPrReset II-163, V-410
lReserved IV-263, V-410
lScreenBits II-164, V-409
lScroll IV-275
lSize IV-274
lUpdate IV-275
lUseSense IV-267

M

macDev V-331
machineType V-6
macMachine II-385
macXLMachine II-385
magentaColor I-158
mapChanged I-126
mapCompact I-126
mapFalse IV-19
mapReadErr IV-18
mapReadOnly I-126
mapTrue IV-19
mask I-146, V-83
matchData V-72
maxIndex IV-264
maxNRel II-22
maxRel II-22
mbResId V-228
mbResID V-230
mChooseMsg I-362
mctID V-231
mctItem V-231
mctReserved V-232
mctRGB1 V-231
mctRGB2 V-232
mctRGB3 V-232
mctRGB4 V-232
mDownMask I-254
mDrawMsg I-362
mdy I-498
memFullErr II-30
memLockedErr II-44
memPurErr II-22
memWZErr II-33
menu V-230
menuData I-345
menuHeight I-345
menuHOH V-229
menuID I-345
menuLeft V-229
menuOH V-229
menuPrgErr V-572
menuProc I-345
menuTitleSave V-229
menuWidth I-345

message I-249
metricSys I-497
midiDataCmd V-483
MidiInitChan V-497
MidiInitChanFilter V-497
MidiInitRawMode V-497
MIDISynthIn V-478
MIDISynthOut V-478
minCBFree II-22
minute II-378
misc II-370
mntLdingZ I-498
mode II-225
modifiers I-249
monaco I-219
month II-378
months I-500
moreMast II-22
mornStr I-497
mouseDown I-249
mouseLoc IV-263
MouseUp I-249
msgHandled V-339
msgIgnored V-339
mSizeMsg I-362
mUpMask I-254
MYD V-290
mySocket II-302

N

nbp II-320
nbpControl II-320
nbpID II-320
nbpSize II-274
nbpTCount II-320
nbpTuple II-320
nDescent I-231
needBits I-224
needsFlush II-215
negZcbFreeErr V-572
networkEvt I-249
networkMask I-254
newProc1 V-91
newProc2 V-91
newProc3 V-91
newProc4 V-91
newProc5 V-91
newProc6 V-91
newSelMsg IV-217
newYork I-219
nextChan V-481
nextControl I-317
nextStub V-482
nextWindow I-276, V-199
nilHandleErr II-33
nis II-321

nLines I-377
noConstraint I-295, 325
noErr I-116
NoErr V-411
noGrowDocProc I-273
noMark I-359
noParity II-251
noScrapErr I-459
NoSuchRsl V-411
noteCmd V-482
noteIcon I-420
noteSynth V-478
notPatBic I-157
notPatCopy I-157
notPatOr I-157
notPatXor I-157
notSrcBic I-157
notSrcCopy I-157
notSrcOr I-157
notSrcXor I-157
nRuns V-261
nStyles V-261
ntEntity II-321
ntLink II-321
ntSocket II-321
ntTuple II-321
nulDev V-331
nullCmd V-482
nullEvent I-249
nullScrap V-264
nullStyle V-261
numEntries V-234
numer I-224
numToString I-489

O

objStr II-298
oddParity II-251
ok I-407
opcodeProc V-91
OpNotImpl V-411
optionKey I-253
outlineBit I-152
ovalProct I-197
owTable I-231
owTLoc I-231

P

packSize V-53
packType V-53
parityErr II-252
pasteDev V-331
patBic I-157
patCopy I-157
patData V-55

patlData V-55
patMap V-55
patOr I-157
patStretch I-148
patType V-55
patXData V-55
patXMap V-55
patXor I-157
patXValid V-55
pauseCmd V-482
pFileName II-151
phaseCmd V-483
pHiliteBit V-62
picFrame I-159
picLParen I-159
picRParen I-159
picSave I-148
picSize I-159
pIdleProc II-151
pixelSize V-53
pixelType V-53
plainDBox I-273
planeBytes V-53
plusCursor I-474
pmAnimated V-154
pmBkColor V-67
pmBkIndex V-67
pmCourteous V-154
pmDataFields V-159
pmDithered V-154
pmEntries V-159
pmExplicit V-154
pmFgColor V-67
pmFgIndex V-67
pmFlags V-67
pmInfo V-159
pmReserved V-53
pmTable V-53
pmTolerant V-154
pmVersion V-53
pnLoc I-148
pnLoc V-50
pnLocHFrac V-50
pnMode I-148
pnMode V-50
pnPat I-148
pnPixPat V-50
pnSize I-148
pnSize V-50
pnVis I-148, V-50
polyBBox I-159
polyPoints I-159
polyProc I-197
polySave I-148
polySize I-159
port I-276, IV-263

portA   II-370
portB   II-370
portBits   I-148
portPixMap   V-50
portRect   I-148, V-50
portVersion   V-50
posCntl   I-329
pPrPort   II-161
PrClose   V-409
PrCloseDoc   V-409
PrClosePage   V-409
PrCtlCall   V-409
PrDrvClose   V-409
PrDrvrDCE   V-409
PrDrvrOpen   V-409
PrDrvrVers   V-409
PrError   V-409
prInfo   II-149
prInfoPT   II-149
PrintDefault   V-409
printX   II-149
prJob   II-149
PrJobDialog   V-409
PrJobMerge   V-409
processor   V-6
procID   I-423
PrOpen   V-409
PrOpenDoc   V-409
PrOpenPage   V-409
propFont   I-232, IV-35
prpFntH   IV-35
prpFntHW   IV-35
prpFntW   IV-35
PrPicFile   V-409
PrSetError   V-409
prStl   II-149
PrStlDialog   V-409
PrValidate   V-409
prXInfo   II-149
purgeProc   II-22
purgePtr   II-22
pushButProc   I-315
putCancel   I-522, 522
putDlgID   I-521, 527
putDrive   I-522
putEject   I-522
putName   I-522
putPicProc   I-197
putSave   I-522
putSave   I-522

Q

qFlags   II-372
qHead   II-372, V-481
qLength   V-481
qLink   II-71, 215

qTail   II-372, V-481
qType   II-71, 215
queue   V-481
quietCmd   V-482

R

radioButProc   I-315
rateCmd   V-483
rDocProc   I-273
rdVerify   II-101, IV-121
recalBack   I-377
recalLines   I-377
rectProc   I-197
red   V-71
redColor   I-158
refCon   I-276, 423, IV-263
reqLData   V-144
reqLsize   V-144
requestNextCmd   V-482
resAttrErr   IV-18
resChanged   I-111
reserved   V-229
resFNotFound   I-116
resLocked   I-111
resNotFound   I-116
resPreload   I-111
resProtected   I-111
resPurgeable   I-111
resSysHeap   I-111
restCmd   V-482
resumeCmd   V-482
rgb   V-136
RGB2CMY   V-174
RGB2HSL   V-174
RGB2HSV   V-174
rgbBkColor   V-50
rgbFgColor   V-50
rgbHiliteColor   V-67
rgbOpColor   V-67
rgnProc   I-197
rgnSave   I-148
rgRslRec   V-412
rmvResFailed   I-116
rowBytes   V-52
rowWords   I-231
rPage   II-149
rPaper   II-149
rRectProc   I-197
rTCClk   III-37
rTCData   III-37
rTCEnb   III-37
runs   V-261
rView   IV-263

S

sampledSynth   V-478
sanFran   I-219
sBSR   IV-253
scAdd   IV-287
SCalcsPointer   V-438
SCalcStep   V-438
SCardChanged   V-438
scComp   IV-287
sCDR   IV-253
scInc   IV-287
SCkCardStatus   V-438
scLoop   IV-287
scMove   IV-287
scNoInc   IV-287
scNOp   IV-287
scrapCount   I-457
scrapHandle   I-457
scrapName   I-457
scrapSize   I-457
scrapState   I-457
ScriptUtil   V-316
scrollBarProc   I-315
scrpAscent   V-266
scrpColor   V-266
scrpFace   V-266
scrpFont   V-266
scrpNStyles   V-265
scrpSize   V-266
scrpStartChar   V-266
scrpStyleTab   V-265
scsiCmd   IV-289
scsiComplete   IV-289
scsiGet   IV-289
scsiMsgIn   V-575
scsiMsgOut   V-575
scsiRBlind   IV-289
scsiRd   IV-252
scsiRead   IV-289
scsiReset   IV-289
scsiSelAtn   V-575
scsiSelect   IV-289
scsiStat   IV-289
scsiWBlind   IV-289
scsiWr   IV-252
scsiWrite   IV-289
sCSR   IV-253
scStop   IV-287
sDDPDstSkt   II-310
sDDPSrcSkt   II-310
sDDPType   II-310
SdeleteSRTRec   V-438
sdInstall   V-587
sDMAtx   IV-253
sdOnDrivers   V-588
sdOnPower   V-588

sdOnRestart   V-588
sdOnUnmount   V-588
sdOSType   V-354
sdPowerOff   V-587
sdRemove   V-587
sdReserved   V-354
sdRestart   V-587
sdRestartOrPower   V-588
sdSlot   V-354
sdSResource   V-354
second   II-378
selectMsg   IV-217
selEnd   I-377
selFlags   IV-263
selPoint   I-377
selRect   I-377
selStart   I-377
sendChk   II-314
SExec   V-438
sExtra   IV-41
sfGetFile   I-519
SFindDevBase   V-438
SFindsInfoRecPtr   V-438
SFindsRsrcPtr   V-438
SFindStruct   V-438
sfPGetFile   I-519
sfPPutFile   I-519
sfPutFile   I-519
SGetBlock   V-438
SGetCString   V-438
SGetDriver   V-438
shadow   I-227
shadowBit   I-152
shiftKey   I-253
shortDDP   II-306
shrtDateFmt   I-497
sICR   IV-253
siDataAreaAddr   V-370
sides   II-215
sIDMArx   IV-253
sIDR   IV-253
siServiceRtPtr   V-370
size   I-224
slopRect   I-332
SmallFractFix2   V-174
smAmharic   V-298
smAppScript   V-313
smArabic   V-297
smArmenian   V-298
smBengali   V-297
smBiDirect   V-313
smBurmese   V-298
smChar1byte   V-307
smChar2byte   V-307
smCharAscii   V-307
smCharEuro   V-307

smCharLeft   V-307
smCharLower   V-307
smCharPunct   V-307
smCharRight   V-307
smCharUpper   V-307
smChinese   V-297
smDevanagari   V-297
smEnabled   V-313
smfontForce   V-313
smForced   V-313
smGeorgian   V-298
smGreek   V-297
smGujarati   V-297
smGurmukhi   V-297
smHebrew   V-297
smHilite   V-308
smIntlForce   V-313
smKanji   V-297
smKannada   V-297
smKeyCache   V-313
smKeyScript   V-313
smKeySwap   V-313
smKhmer   V-298
smKorean   V-297
smLaotian   V-298
smLeftCaret   V-308
smMalayalam   V-297
smMaldivian   V-298
smMaskAll   V-311
smMaskAscii   V-311
smMaskNative   V-311
smMongolian   V-298
smMunged   V-313
smOriya   V-297
smPrint   V-313
smPunctBlank   V-307
smPunctNormal   V-307
smPunctNumber   V-307
smPunctSymbol   V-307
sMR   IV-253
smReserved1   V-297
smRightCaret   V-308
smRoman   V-297
smRussian   V-297
smScriptCreator   V-312
smScriptDate   V-312
smScriptEnabled   V-312
smScriptfile   V-312
smScriptIcon   V-312
smScriptJust   V-312
smScriptKeys   V-312
smScriptMunged   V-312
smScriptName   V-313
smScriptNumber   V-312
smScriptPrint   V-312
smScriptRedraw   V-312

smScriptRight   V-312
smScriptRsvd1   V-312
smScriptRsvd2   V-312
smScriptRsvd3   V-312
smScriptRsvd4   V-312
smScriptSort   V-312
smScriptSysFond   V-312
smScriptTrap   V-312
smScriptVersion   V-312
smSindhi   V-298
smSinhalese   V-297
smSlavic   V-298
smSysRef   V-313
smSysScript   V-313
smTamil   V-297
smTelugu   V-297
smThai   V-298
smTibetan   V-298
smTransAscii   V-311
smTransCase   V-311
smTransLower   V-311
smTransNative   V-311
smTransUpper   V-311
smUninterp   V-298
smVersion   V-313
smVietnamese   V-298
SNextRsrc   V-438
SNextTypesRsrc   V-438
snScriptRsvd5   V-312
sOCR   IV-253
SOffsetData   V-438
sound1   I-424
sound1Phase   II-227
sound1Rate   II-227
sound1Wave   II-227
sound2   I-424
sound2Phase   II-227
sound2Rate   II-227
sound2Wave   II-227
sound3   I-424
sound3Phase   II-227
sound3Rate   II-227
sound3Wave   II-227
sound4   I-424
sound4Phase   II-227
sound4Rate   II-227
sound4Wave   II-227
soundCmd   V-483
spareFlag   I-276, V-199
sparePtr   II-22
spExtra   I-148, V-50
sPrDrvr   II-162
SPrimaryInit   V-438
SPtrToSlot   V-438
SPutPRAMRec   V-438
SQAddr   V-426

SQLink   V-426
SQParm   V-426
SQPrio   V-426
SQType   V-426
srcBic   I-157
srcCopy   I-157
srcOr   I-157
srcXor   I-157
SReadByte   V-438
SReadDrvrName   V-438
SReadFHeader   V-438
SReadInfo   V-438
SReadLong   V-438
SReadPBSize   V-438
SReadPRAMRec   V-438
SReadStruct   V-438
SReadWord   V-438
sRESET   IV-253
SRsrcInfo   V-438
SSearchSRt   V-438
sSER   IV-253
st0   I-500
st1   I-500
st2   I-500
st3   I-500
st4   I-500
stages   I-424
star   II-320
stAscent   V-262
stColor   V-262
stCount   V-262
sTCR   IV-253
stdFile   I-483, IV-67
sTDMA   IV-253
stdState   IV-49
stFace   V-262
stFont   V-262
stHeight   V-262
stop10   II-251
stop15   II-251
stop20   II-251
stopIcon   I-420
stringToNum   I-489
strucRgn   I-276, V-199
stSize   V-262
style   IV-41
styleTab   V-261
subOver   V-61
subPin   V-61
SUpdateSRT   V-438
supDay   V-291
supMonth   V-291
suppressDay   I-500
supWeek   V-291
supYear   V-291
swMode   II-225

swOverrunErr   II-254
symbol   I-219
syncCmd   V-482
systemFont   I-219
systemVersion   V-6
sysVRefNum   V-6

T

tabData   IV-41
tabFont   IV-41
tabSize   IV-41
taliesin   I-219
TEaddSize   V-281
TEdoAll   V-281
TEdoColor   V-281
TEdoFace   V-281
TEdoFont   V-281
TEdoSize   V-281
teJustCenter   I-377
teJustLeft   I-377
teJustRight   I-377
teLength   I-377
teRefCon   V-261
TEReserved   V-264
terminateMsg   IV-218
testCntl   I-329
textH   I-408
textMenuProc   I-362
textProc   I-197
tgBuffCode   II-214
thousSep   I-497
thumbCntl   I-329
tickleCmd   V-482
tidValid   II-314
timbreCmd   V-483
time1Suff   I-497
time2Suff   I-497
time3Suff   I-497
time4Suff   I-497
time5Suff   I-497
time6Suff   I-497
time7Suff   I-497
time8Suff   I-497
timeCycle   I-497
timeFmt   I-497
times   I-219
timeSep   I-497
title   I-423
titleHandle   I-276, V-199
titleWidth   I-276, V-199
tmAddr   IV-299
tmCount   IV-299
toronto   I-219
track   II-215
transparent   V-61
trFunc   I-483

trFunct   IV-67
triplets   II-225
true32b   V-592
tsColor   V-265
tsFace   V-265
tsFont   V-265
tsSize   V-265
tupleEnum   II-320
tupleMax   II-320
tupleName   II-320
tupleNet   II-320
tupleNode   II-320
tupleSkt   II-320
twoSideFmt   II-215
txFace   I-148, 377, V-50
txFont   I-148, 377, V-50
txMeasProc   I-197
txMode   I-148, 377, V-50
txSize   I-148, 377, V-50
tyBkFree   II-24
tyBkNReal   II-24
tyBkRel   II-24
typeStr   II-298

U

ulineBit   I-152
ulOffset   I-227
ulShadow   I-227
ulThick   I-227
undoDev   V-331
UnimplCoreRoutine   V-316
unused   I-227
updateDev   V-331
updateEvt   I-249
updateMask   I-254
updateRgn   V-199
updatRgn   I-276
useAsync   II-305
useATalk   II-305
usedFam   IV-41
useFree   II-305
userBytes   II-288
userHandle   IV-264
userInfo   V-481, 482
userState   IV-49
useWFont   I-315

V

valid   II-370
value   V-136
vAxisOnly   I-295, 325
vblAddr   II-350
vblCount   II-350
vblPhase   II-350

vcbAlBlkSiz II-125, IV-176
vcbAlBlst II-125
vcbAllocPtr IV-176
vcbAtrb II-125
vcbBufAdr II-125
vcbBufAdr IV-176
vcbClpSiz II-125
vcbClpSiz IV-176
vcbCrDate II-125
vcbCTAlBks IV-177
vcbCTClpSiz IV-176
vcbCtlBuf IV-177
vcbCtlCSiz IV-177
vcbCTRef IV-177
vcbDirBlk II-125, IV-176
vcbDirCnt IV-176
vcbDirIDM IV-177
vcbDirIndex II-125, IV-176
vcbDirSt II-125
vcbDRefNum II-125, IV-176
vcbDrvNum II-125, IV-176
vcbFilCnt IV-176
vcbFLags II-125
vcbFndrInfo IV-177
vcbFreeBks II-125, IV-176
vcbFSID II-125, IV-176
vcblLn II-125
vcbLsBkUp II-125
vcbLsMod IV-176
vcbMAdr II-125, IV-176
vcbMLen II-125, IV-176
vcbNmAlBlks IV-176
vcbNmBlks II-125
vcbNmFls II-125
vcbNmRtDirs IV-176
vcbNxtCNID IV-176
vcbNxtFNum II-125
vcbOffsM IV-177
vcbSigWord II-125
vcbVBMCSiz IV-177
vcbVBMSt IV-176
vcbVCSize IV-177
vcbVN II-125, IV-176
vcbVolBkUp IV-176
vcbVRefNum II-125, IV-176
vcbVSeqNum IV-176
vcbWrCnt IV-176
vcbXTAlBks IV-177
vcbXTClpSiz IV-176
vcbXTRef IV-177
vcvbAlBlSt IV-176
venice I-219
verArabia I-499

verAustralia I-499
verBelgiumLux I-499
verBritain I-499
verCyprus I-499
verDenmark I-499
verFinland I-499
verFrance I-499
verFrCanada I-499
verFrSwiss I-499
verGermany I-499
verGreece I-499
verGrSwiss I-499
verIceland I-499
verIsrael I-499
verItaly I-499
verJapan I-499
verMalta I-499
verNetherlands I-499
verNorway I-499
verPortugal I-499
version I-519, I-527
versNum II-58
verSpain I-499
verSweden I-499
verTurkey I-499
verUS I-499
verYugoslavia I-499
vFactor IV-41
viewRect I-377
visible I-276, 423, IV-263, V-199
visRgn I-148, V-50
volClik II-370
vOutput IV-41
vPage2 III-20
vRefNum I-519, I-527
vrefNum II-58
vRes V-53
vScroll IV-263
vSndEnb III-21
vSndPg2 III-21
vSound III-21
vSW III-27
vType II-373
vTypErr II-351

W

wait V-481
waitCmd V-482
wakeUpCmd V-482
watchCursor I-474
waveBytes II-228
waveTableCmd V-483
waveTableSynth V-478
wCalcRgns I-299
wContentColor V-204

wCReserved V-202
wCSeed V-202
wDev II-152
wDispose I-299
wDraw I-299
wDrawGIcon I-299
wFrameColor V-204
wGrow I-299
what I-249
when I-249
where I-249
wHiliteColor V-204
wHit I-299
whiteColor I-158
widMax I-173
wInContent I-300
window I-408
windowDefProc I-276, V-199
windowKind I-276, V-199
windowPic I-276, V-199
wInDrag I-300
wInGoAway I-300
wInGrow I-300
wInZoomIn IV-50
wInZoomOut IV-50
wNew I-299
wNoHit I-299
wordBreak I-377
writeProt II-215
wTabHandle IV-32
wTextColor V-204
wTitleBarColor V-204

X, Y, Z

xOffWasSent II-254
xppTfRNum V-531
xppUnitNum V-531
XRslRg V-412
YDM V-290
year II-378
yellowColor I-158
ymd I-498
YRslRg V-412
zcbFree II-22
zeroCycle V-290
zoneSize II-45
zoneStr II-298

APPENDIX A: ROUTINES THAT MAY MOVE OR PURGE MEMORY

This appendix lists all the routines that may move or purge blocks in the heap. As described in *Inside Macintosh,* Volume II, chapter 1, calling these routines may cause problems if a handle has been dereferenced. None of these routines may be called from within an interrupt, such as in a completion routine or a VBL task.

The Pascal name of each routine is shown, except for a few cases where there's no Pascal interface corresponding to a particular trap; in those cases, the trap macro name is shown instead (without its initial underscore character).

ActivatePalette
ADBReInit
AddComp
AddResMenu
AddSearch
Alert
AllocCrsr
AppendMenu
ATPAddRsp
ATPCloseSocket
ATPGetRequest
ATPLoad
ATPOpenSocket
ATPReqCancel
ATPRequest
ATPResponse
ATPRspCancel
ATPSndRequest
ATPSndRsp
ATPUnload
BackColor
BackPat
BackPixPat
BeginUpdate
BringToFront
Button
CalcMenuSize
CalcVis
CalcVisBehind
CautionAlert
Chain
ChangedResource
Char2Pixel
CharWidth
CheckItem
CheckUpdate
ClipAbove
ClipRect

CloseCPort
CloseDialog
ClosePicture
ClosePoly
ClosePort
CloseResFile
CloseRgn
CloseWindow
CMY2RGB
Color2Index
CompactMem
Control
CopyBits
CopyMask
CopyPalette
CopyRgn
CouldAlert
CouldDialog
CreateResFile
CStr2Dec
CTab2Palette
DDPCloseSocket
DDPOpenSocket
DDPRdCancel
DDPRead
DDPWrite
Dec2Str
DelComp
DelMenuItem
DelSearch
DialogSelect
DIBadMount
DiffRgn
DIFormat
DILoad
DiskEject
DispMCInfo
DisposCIcon

DisposCTable
DisposDialog
DisposeControl
DisposeMenu
DisposePalette
DisposeRgn
DisposeWindow
DisposGDevice
DisposHandle
DisposPixMap
DisposPixPat
DisposPtr
DIUnload
DIVerify
DIZero
DlgCopy
DlgCut
DlgDelete
DlgPaste
DragControl
DragGrayRgn
DragWindow
Draw1Control
DrawChar
DrawDialog
DrawGrowIcon
DrawJust
DrawMenuBar
DrawNew
DrawPicture
DrawString
DrawText
DriveStatus
DrvrInstall
DrvrRemove
Eject
EmptyHandle
EndUpdate

EraseArc
EraseOval
ErasePalette
ErasePoly
EraseRect
EraseRgn
EraseRoundRect
EventAvail
ExitToShell
FillArc
FillCArc
FillCOval
FillCPoly
FillCRect
FillCRgn
FillCRoundRect
FillOval
FillPoly
FillRect
FillRgn
FillRoundRect
FindControl
FindDItem
FindWord
Fix2SmallFract
FlashMenuBar
FlushVol
FMSwapFont
Font2Script
FontMetrics
FontScript
ForeColor
FrameArc
FrameOval
FramePoly
FrameRect
FrameRgn
FrameRoundRect
FreeAlert
FreeDialog
FreeMem
Get1IndResource
Get1IndType
Get1NamedResource
Get1Resource
GetAuxCtl
GetCCursor
GetCIcon
GetClip
GetColor
GetCTable
GetCursor

GetDCtlEntry
GetDItem
GetFNum
GetFontInfo
GetFontName
GetGrayRgn
GetIcon
GetIndPattern
GetIndResource
GetIndString
GetKeys
GetMCInfo
GetMenu
GetMenuBar
GetMouse
GetNamedResource
GetNewControl
GetNewCWindow
GetNewDialog
GetNewMBar
GetNewPalette
GetNewWindow
GetNextEvent
GetPattern
GetPicture
GetPixPat
GetResource
GetScrap
GetString
GetStylHandle
GetStylScrap
GetSubTable
GrowWindow
HandAndHand
HandToHand
HideControl
HideDItem
HideWindow
HiliteControl
HiliteMenu
HiliteText
HiliteWindow
HSL2RGB
HSV2RGB
InitAllPacks
InitApplZone
InitCPort
InitFonts
InitGDevice
InitGraf
InitMenus
InitPack

InitPalettes
InitPort
InitPort
InitPRAMRecs
InitProcMenu
InitResources
InitSDeclMgr
InitsRsrcTable
InitWindows
InitZone
InsertMenu
InsertResMenu
InsetRgn
InsMenuItem
IntlScript
InvalRect
InvalRgn
InvertArc
InvertOval
InvertPoly
InvertRect
InvertRgn
InvertRoundRect
IUCompString
IUDatePString
IUDateString
IUEqualString
IUGetIntl
IUMagIDString
IUMagString
IUMetric
IUSetIntl
IUTimePString
IUTimeString
KeyScript
KillControls
KillPicture
KillPoly
LAPCloseProtocol
LAPOpenProtocol
LAPRdCancel
LAPRead
LAPWrite
Launch
Line
LineTo
LoadResource
LoadScrap
LoadSeg
MakeITable
MapRgn
MeasureJust

MeasureText	PaintRgn	RecoverHandle
MenuKey	PaintRoundRect	RectRgn
MenuSelect	Palette2CTab	ReleaseResource
ModalDialog	ParamText	ResrvMem
MoreMasters	PBControl	Restart
MoveControl	PBEject	RGB2CMY
MoveHHi	PBFlushVol	RGB2HSL
MoveWindow	PBMountVol	RGB2HSV
MPPClose	PBOffLine	RGBBackColor
MPPOpen	PBOpen	RGBForeColor
Munger	PBOpenRF	RGetResource
NBPConfirm	PBStatus	RmveResource
NBPExtract	PenNormal	RsrcZoneInit
NBPLoad	PenPat	SaveOld
NBPLookup	PenPixPat	ScrollRect
NBPRegister	PicComment	SectRgn
NBPRemove	Pixel2Char	SelectWindow
NBPUnload	PlotCIcon	SelIText
NewCDialog	PlotIcon	SendBehind
NewControl	PMBackColor	SerClrBrk
NewCWindow	PMForeColor	SerGetBrk
NewDialog	PrClose	SerHShake
NewEmptyHandle	PrCloseDoc	SerReset
NewGDevice	PrClosePage	SerSetBrk
NewHandle	PrCtlCall	SerSetBuf
NewMenu	PrDrvrClose	SerStatus
NewPalette	PrDrvrDCE	SetApplBase
NewPixMap	PrDrvrOpen	SetCCursor
NewPixPat	PrDrvrVers	SetClip
NewPort	PrError	SetCPixel
NewPtr	PrGeneral	SetCTitle
NewRgn	PrintDefault	SetCtlColor
NewString	PrJobDialog	SetCtlMax
NewWindow	PrJobMerge	SetCtlMin
NoteAlert	PrOpen	SetCtlValue
NumToString	PrOpenDoc	SetDeskCPat
OpenCPicture	PrOpenPage	SetDItem
OpenCPort	PrPicFile	SetEmptyRgn
OpenDeskAcc	PrSetError	SetFontLock
OpenPicture	PrStlDialog	SetHandleSize
OpenPixMap	PrValidate	SetItem
OpenPoly	PStr2Dec	SetItemIcon
OpenPort	PtrAndHand	SetItemMark
OpenResFile	PtrToHand	SetItemStyle
OpenRFPerm	PtrToXHand	SetIText
OpenRgn	PurgeMem	SetMCInfo
PaintArc	PutScrap	SetPtrSize
PaintBehind	RAMSDClose	SetRectRgn
PaintOne	RAMSDOpen	SetResInfo
PaintOval	RealColor	SetString
PaintPoly	RealFont	SetStylHandle
PaintRect	ReallocHandle	SetTagBuffer

SetWinColor
SetWTitle
sExec
SFGetFile
SFPGetFile
SFPPutFile
SFPutFile
sGetBlock
sGetcString
sGetDriver
ShowControl
ShowDItem
ShowHide
ShowWindow
ShutDwnInstall
ShutDwnRemove
SizeControl
SizeWindow
SmallFract2Fix
SndAddModifier
SndDisposeChannel
SndNewChannel
sPrimaryInit
StartSound
Status
StdArc
StdBits
StdComment
StdLine
StdOval
StdPoly
StdPutPic
StdRect
StdRgn
StdRRect
StdText
StdTxMeas
StillDown
StopAlert
StopSound
StringToNum
StringWidth
SysBeep
SysError
SystemClick
SystemEdit
SystemMenu
TEActivate
TEAutoView
TECalText
TEClick
TECopy

TECut
TEDeactivate
TEDelete
TEDispose
TEFromScrap
TEGetHeight
TEGetOffset
TEGetPoint
TEGetStyle
TEGetText
TEIdle
TEInit
TEInsert
TEKey
TENew
TEPaste
TEPinScroll
TEReplaceStyle
TEScroll
TESelView
TESetJust
TESetSelect
TESetStyle
TESetText
TestControl
TEStylInsert
TEStylNew
TEStylPaste
TEToScrap
TEUpdate
TextBox
TextWidth
TickCount
TrackBox
TrackControl
TrackGoAway
Transliterate
UnionRgn
UnloadScrap
UnloadSeg
UpdtControl
UpdtDialog
ValidRect
ValidRgn
WaitMouseUp
XorRgn
ZeroScrap
ZoomWindow

APPENDIX B: SYSTEM TRAPS

This appendix lists the trap macros for the Toolbox and Operating System routines and their corresponding trap word values in hexadecimal. The "Name" column gives the trap macro name (without its initial underscore character). In those cases where the name of the equivalent Pascal call is different, the Pascal name appears indented under the main entry. The routines in Macintosh packages are listed under the macros they invoke after pushing a routine selector onto the stack; the routine selector follows the Pascal routine name in parentheses.

There are two tables. The first is ordered alphabetically by name; the second is ordered numerically by trap number, for use when debugging. The trap number is the last two digits of the trap word unless the trap word begins with A9, in which case the trap number is 1 followed by the last two digits of the trap word, or AA, in which case the trap number is 2 followed by the last two digits of the trap word.

Note: The Operating System Utility routines GetTrapAddress and SetTrapAddress take a trap number as a parameter, not a trap word.

Warning: Traps that aren't currently used by the system are reserved for future use.

Name	Trap word	Name	Trap word
ActivatePalette	AA94	BitTst	A85D
ADBOp	A07C	BitXor	A859
ADBReInit	A07B	BlockMove	A02E
AddComp	AA3B	BringToFront	A920
AddDrive	A04E	Button	A974
(internal use only)		CalcCMask	AA4F
AddPt	A87E	CalcMask	A838
AddResMenu	A94D	CalcMenuSize	A948
AddResource	A9AB	CalcVBehind	A90A
AddSearch	AA3A	CalcVisBehind	
Alert	A985	CalcVis	A909
Allocate	A010	CautionAlert	A988
PBAllocate		Chain	A9F3
AllocCursor	AA1D	ChangedResource	A9AA
AngleFromSlope	A8C4	CharExtra	AA23
AnimateEntry	AA99	CharWidth	A88D
AnimatePalette	AA9A	CheckItem	A945
AppendMenu	A933	CheckUpdate	A911
AttachVBL	A071	ClearMenuBar	A934
BackColor	A863	ClipAbove	A90B
BackPat	A87C	ClipRect	A87B
BackPixPat	AA0B	Close	A001
BeginUpdate	A922	PBClose	
BitAnd	A858	CloseCPort	A87D
BitClr	A85F	CloseDeskAcc	A9B7
BitNot	A85A	CloseDialog	A982
BitOr	A85B	ClosePgon	A8CC
BitSet	A85E	ClosePoly	
BitShift	A85C	ClosePicture	A8F4

Name	Trap word	Name	Trap word
ClosePort	A87D	DisposDialog	A983
CloseResFile	A99A	DisposGDevice	AA30
CloseRgn	A8DB	DisposHandle	A023
CloseWindow	A92D	DisposMenu	A932
CmpString	A03C	DisposeMenu	
EqualString		DisposePalette	AA93
ColorBit	A864	DisposPixMap	AA04
Color2Index	AA33	DisposPixPat	AA08
CompactMem	A04C	DisposPtr	A01F
Control	A004	DisposRgn	A8D9
PBControl		DisposeRgn	
CopyBits	A8EC	DisposWindow	A914
CopyMask	A817	DisposeWindow	
CopyPixMap	AA05	DoVBLTask	A072
CopyPixPat	AA09	DragControl	A967
CopyRgn	A8DC	DragGrayRgn	A905
CouldAlert	A989	DragTheRgn	A926
CouldDialog	A979	DragWindow	A925
Count1Resources	A80D	Draw1Control	A96D
Count1Types	A81C	DrawChar	A883
CountADBs	A077	DrawControls	A969
CountMItems	A950	DrawDialog	A981
CountResources	A99C	DrawGrowIcon	A904
CountTypes	A99E	DrawMenuBar	A937
Create	A008	DrawNew	A90F
PBCreate		DrawPicture	A8F6
CreateResFile	A9B1	DrawString	A884
CTab2Palette	AA9F	DrawText	A885
CurResFile	A994	DrvrInstall	A03D
Date2Secs	A9C7	(internal use only)	
Delay	A03B	DrvrRemove	A03E
DelComp	AA4D	(internal use only)	
Delete	A009	DTInstall	A082
PBDelete		Ejcct	A017
DeleteMenu	A936	PBEject	
DelMCEntries	AA60	Elems68K	A9EC
DelMenuItem	A952	EmptyHandle	A02B
DelSearch	AA4C	EmptyRect	A8AE
DeltaPoint	A94F	EmptyRgn	A8E2
Dequeue	A96E	EnableItem	A939
DetachResource	A992	EndUpdate	A923
DialogSelect	A980	Enqueue	A96F
DiffRgn	A8E6	EqualPt	A881
DisableItem	A93A	EqualRect	A8A6
DispMCInfo	AA63	EqualRgn	A8E3
DisposCCursor	AA26	EraseArc	A8C0
DisposCIcon	AA25	EraseOval	A8B9
DisposControl	A955	ErasePoly	A8C8
DisposeControl		EraseRect	A8A3
DisposCTable	AA24	EraseRgn	A8D4

Name	Trap word	Name	Trap word
EraseRoundRect	A8B2	FreeAlert	A98A
ErrorSound	A98C	FreeDialog	A97A
EventAvail	A971	FreeMem	A01C
ExitToShell	A9F4	FrontWindow	A924
FillArc	A8C2	GetADBInfo	A079
FillCArc	AA11	GetAppParms	A9F5
FillCOval	AA0F	GetAuxCtl	AA44
FillCPoly	AA13	GetAuxWin	AA42
FillCRect	AA0E	GetBackColor	AA1A
FillCRgn	AA12	GetCCursor	AA1B
FillCRoundRect	AA10	GetCIcon	AA1E
FillOval	A8BB	GetClip	A87A
FillPoly	A8CA	GetCPixel	AA17
FillRect	A8A5	GetCRefCon	A95A
FillRgn	A8D6	GetCTable	AA18
FillRoundRect	A8B4	GetCTitle	A95E
FindControl	A96C	GetCtlAction	A96A
FindDItem	A984	GetCtlValue	A960
FindWindow	A92C	GetCTSeed	AA28
Fix2Frac	A841	GetCursor	A9B9
Fix2Long	A840	GetCVariant	A809
Fix2X	A843	GetCWMgrPort	AA48
FixAtan2	A818	GetDefaultStartup	A07D
FixDiv	A84D	GetDeviceList	AA29
FixMul	A868	GetDItem	A98D
FixRatio	A869	GetEntryColor	AA9B
FixRound	A86C	GetEntryUsage	AA9D
FlashMenuBar	A94C	GetEOF	A011
FlushEvents	A032	PBGetEOF	
FlushFile	A045	GetFileInfo	A00C
PBFlushFile		PBGetFInfo	
FlushVol	A013	GetFName	A8FF
PBFlushVol		GetFontName	
FMSwapFont	A901	GetFNum	A900
FontMetrics	A835	GetFontInfo	A88B
ForeColor	A862	GetForeColor	AA19
FP68K	A9EB	GetFPos	A018
Frac2Fix	A842	PBGetFPos	
Frac2X	A845	GetGDevice	AA32
FracCos	A847	GetHandleSize	A025
FracDiv	A84B	GetIcon	A9BB
FracMul	A84A	GetIndADB	A078
FracSin	A848	GetIndResource	A99D
FracSqrt	A849	GetIndType	A99F
FrameArc	A8BE	GetItem	A946
FrameOval	A8B7	GetItemCmd	A84E
FramePoly	A8C6	GetIText	A990
FrameRect	A8A1	GetItmIcon	A93F
FrameRgn	A8D2	GetItemIcon	
FrameRoundRect	A8B0		

Name	Trap word	Name	Trap word
GetItmMark	A943	GetSubTable	AA37
GetItemMark		GetTrapAddress	A146
GetItmStyle	A941	GetVideoDefault	A080
GetItemStyle		GetVol	A014
GetKeys	A976	PBGetVol	
GetMainDevice	AA2A	GetVolInfo	A007
GetMaxCtl	A962	PBGetVInfo	
GetCtlMax		GetWindowPic	A92F
GetMaxDevice	AA27	GetWMgrPort	A910
GetMCEntry	AA64	GetWRefCon	A917
GetMCInfo	AA61	GetWTitle	A919
GetMenuBar	A93B	GetWVariant	A80A
GetMHandle	A949	GetZone	A11A
GetMinCtl	A961	GlobalToLocal	A871
GetCtlMin		GrafDevice	A872
GetMouse	A972	GrowWindow	A92B
GetNamedResource	A9A1	HandAndHand	A9E4
GetNewControl	A9BE	HandleZone	A126
GetNewCWindow	AA46	HandToHand	A9E1
GetNewDialog	A97C	HClrRBit	A068
GetNewMBar	A9C0	HFSDispatch	A260
GetNewPalette	AA92	OpenWD	(1)
GetNewWindow	A9BD	CloseWD	(2)
GetNextDevice	AA2B	CatMove	(5)
GetNextEvent	A970	DirCreate	(6)
Get1IxResource	A80E	GetWDInfo	(7)
Get1IndResource		GetFCBInfo	(8)
Get1IxType	A80F	GetCatInfo	(9)
Get1IndType		SetCatInfo	(10)
Get1NamedResource	A820	SetVolInfo	(11)
Get1Resource	A81F	LockRng	(16)
GetOSDefault	A084	UnlockRng	(17)
GetOSEvent	A031	HGetState	A069
GetPalette	AA96	HideControl	A958
GetPattern	A9B8	HideCursor	A852
GetPen	A89A	HideDItem	A827
GetPenState	A898	HidePen	A896
GetPicture	A9BC	HideWindow	A916
GetPixel	A865	HiliteColor	AA22
GetPixPat	AA0C	HiliteControl	A95D
GetPort	A874	HiliteMenu	A938
GetPtrSize	A021	HiliteWindow	A91C
GetResAttrs	A9A6	HiWord	A86A
GetResFileAttrs	A9F6	HLock	A029
GetResInfo	A9A8	HNoPurge	A04A
GetResource	A9A0	HomeResFile	A9A4
GetRMenu	A9BF	HPurge	A049
GetMenu		HSetRBit	A067
GetScrap	A9FD	HSetState	A06A
GetString	A9BA	HUnlock	A02A

Name	Trap word	Name	Trap word
Index2Color	AA34	LineTo	A891
InfoScrap	A9F9	LoadResource	A9A2
InitAllPacks	A9E6	LoadSeg	A9F0
InitApplZone	A02C	LocalToGlobal	A870
InitCport	AA01	LodeScrap	A9FB
InitCursor	A850	LoadScrap	
InitDialogs	A97B	Long2Fix	A83F
InitFonts	A8FE	LongMul	A867
InitGDevice	AA2E	LoWord	A86B
InitGraf	A86E	MakeITable	AA39
InitMenus	A930	MakeRGBPat	AA0D
InitPack	A9E5	MapPoly	A8FC
InitPalettes	AA90	MapPt	A8F9
InitPort	A86D	MapRect	A8FA
InitProcMenu	A808	MapRgn	A8FB
InitQueue	A016	MaxApplZone	A063
FInitQueue		MaxBlock	A061
InitResources	A995	MaxMem	A11D
InitUtil	A03F	MaxSizeRsrc	A821
InitWindows	A912	MeasureText	A837
InitZone	A019	MenuChoice	AA66
InsertMenu	A935	MenuKey	A93E
InsertResMenu	A951	MenuSelect	A93D
InsetRect	A8A9	ModalDialog	A991
InsetRgn	A8E1	MoreMasters	A036
InsMenuItem	A826	MountVol	A00F
InternalWait	A07F	PBMountVol	
SetTimeout	(0)	Move	A894
GetTimeout	(1)	MoveControl	A959
InvalRect	A928	MoveHHi	A064
InvalRgn	A927	MovePortTo	A877
InverRect	A8A4	MoveTo	A893
InvertRect		MoveWindow	A91B
InverRgn	A8D5	Munger	A9E0
InvertRgn		NewCDialog	AA4B
InverRoundRect	A8B3	NewControl	A954
InvertRoundRect		NewCWindow	AA45
InvertArc	A8C1	NewDialog	A97D
InvertColor	AA35	NewEmptyHandle	A066
InvertOval	A8BA	NewGDevice	AA2F
InvertPoly	A8C9	NewHandle	A122
IsDialogEvent	A97F	NewMenu	A931
KeyTrans	A9C3	NewPalette	AA91
KillControls	A956	NewPixMap	AA03
KillIO	A006	NewPixPat	AA07
PBKillIO		NewPtr	A11E
KillPicture	A8F5	NewRgn	A8D8
KillPoly	A8CD	NewString	A906
Launch	A9F2	NewWindow	A913
Line	A892	NoteAlert	A987

Name	Trap word		Name	Trap word
ObscureCursor	A856		Pack2	A9E9
Offline	A035		DIBadMount	(0)
PBOffline			DIFormat	(6)
OffsetPoly	A8CE		DILoad	(2)
OffsetRect	A8A8		DIUnload	(4)
OfsetRgn	A8E0		DIVerify	(8)
OffsetRgn			DIZero	(10)
OpColor	AA21		Pack3	A9EA
Open	A000		SFGetFile	(2)
PBOpen			SFPGetFile	(4)
OpenCport	AA00		SFPPutFile	(3)
OpenDeskAcc	A9B6		SFPutFile	(1)
OpenPicture	A8F3		Pack4	A9EB
OpenPoly	A8CB		Pack5	A9EC
OpenPort	A86F		Pack6	A9ED
OpenResFile	A997		IUDatePString	(14)
OpenRF	A00A		IUDateString	(0)
PBOpenRF			IUGetIntl	(6)
OpenRFPerm	A9C4		IUMagIDString	(12)
OpenRgn	A8DA		IUMagString	(10)
OSEventAvail	A030		IUMetric	(4)
Pack0	A9E7		IUSetIntl	(8)
LActivate	(0)		IUTimePString	(16)
LAddColumn	(4)		IUTimeString	(2)
LAddRow	(8)		Pack7	A9EE
LAddToCell	(12)		NumToString	(0)
LAutoScroll	(16)		StringToNum	(1)
LCellSize	(20)		PStr2Dec	(2)
LClick	(24)		Dec2Str	(3)
LClrCell	(28)		CStr2Dec	(4)
LDelColumn	(32)		Pack8	A816
LDelRow	(36)		Pack9	A82B
LDispose	(40)		Pack10	A82C
LDoDraw	(44)		Pack11	A82D
LDraw	(48)		(Pack 8–11 reserved for future use)	
LFind	(52)		Pack12	A82E
LGetCell	(56)		Fix2SmallFract	(1)
LGetSelect	(60)		SmallFract2Fix	(2)
LLastClick	(64)		CMY2RGB	(3)
LNew	(68)		RGB2CMY	(4)
LNextCell	(72)		HSL2RGB	(5)
LRect	(76)		RGB2HSL	(6)
LScroll	(80)		HSV2RGB	(7)
LSearch	(84)		RGB2HSV	(8)
LSetCell	(88)		GetColor	(9)
LSetSelect	(92)		Pack13	A82F
LSize	(96)		Pack14	A830
LUpdate	(100)		Pack15	A831
Pack1	A9E8		(Pack 13–15 reserved for future use)	
(reserved for future use)			PackBits	A8CF

Name	Trap word	Name	Trap word
PaintArc	A8BF	RectRgn	A8DF
PaintBehind	A90D	ReleaseResource	A9A3
PaintOne	A90C	RelString	A050
PaintOval	A8B8	Rename	A00B
PaintPoly	A8C7	PBRename	
PaintRect	A8A2	ResError	A9AF
PaintRgn	A8D3	ReserveEntry	AA3E
PaintRoundRect	A8B1	ResrvMem	A040
Palette2CTab	AAA0	RestoreEntries	AA4A
ParamText	A98B	RGBBackColor	AA15
PenMode	A89C	RGBForeColor	AA14
PenNormal	A89E	RGetResource	A80C
PenPat	A89D	RmveResource	A9AD
PenPixPat	AA0A	RsrcMapEntry	A9C5
PenSize	A89B	RsrcZoneInit	A996
PicComment	A8F2	RstFilLock	A042
PinRect	A94E	PBRstFLock	
PlotCIcon	AA1F	SaveEntries	AA49
PlotIcon	A94B	SaveOld	A90E
PmBackColor	AA98	ScalePt	A8F8
PmForeColor	AA97	ScriptUtil	A8B5
PopUpMenuSelect	A80B	smFontScript	(0)
PortSize	A876	smIntlScript	(2)
PostEvent	A02F	smKybdScript	(4)
PPostEvent	A12F	smFont2Script	(6)
PrGlue	A8FD	smGetEnvirons	(8)
ProtectEntry	AA3D	smSetEnvirons	(10)
Pt2Rect	A8AC	smGetScript	(12)
PtInRect	A8AD	smSetScript	(14)
PtInRgn	A8E8	smCharByte	(16)
PtrAndHand	A9EF	smCharType	(18)
PtrToHand	A9E3	smPixel2Char	(20)
PtrToXHand	A9E2	smChar2Pixel	(22)
PtrZone	A148	smTranslit	(24)
PtToAngle	A8C3	smFindWord	(26)
PurgeMem	A04D	smHiliteText	(28)
PurgeSpace	A062	smDrawJust	(30)
PutScrap	A9FE	smMeasureJust	(32)
QDError	AA40	ScrollRect	A8EF
Random	A861	SCSIDispatch	A815
RDrvrInstall	A04F	SCSIReset	(0)
(internal use only)		SCSIGet	(1)
Read	A002	SCSISelect	(2)
PBRead		SCSICmd	(3)
ReadDateTime	A039	SCSIComplete	(4)
RealColor	AA36	SCSIRead	(5)
RealFont	A902	SCSIWrite	(6)
ReallocHandle	A027	SCSIInstall	(7)
RecoverHandle	A128	SCSIRBlind	(8)
RectInRgn	A8E9	SCSIWBlind	(9)

Name	Trap word	Name	Trap word
SCSIStat	(10)	SetHandleSize	A024
SCSISelAtn	(11)	SetItem	A947
SCSIMsgIn	(12)	SetItemCmd	A84F
SCSIMsgOut	(13)	SetIText	A98F
Secs2Date	A9C6	SetItmIcon	A940
SectRect	A8AA	SetItemIcon	
SectRgn	A8E4	SetItmMark	A944
SeedCFill	AA50	SetItemMark	
SeedFill	A839	SetItmStyle	A942
SelectWindow	A91F	SetItemStyle	
SelIText	A97E	SetMaxCtl	A965
SendBehind	A921	SetCtlMax	
SetADBInfo	A07A	SetMCEntries	AA65
SetAppBase	A057	SetMCInfo	AA62
SetApplBase		SetMenuBar	A93C
SetApplLimit	A02D	SetMFlash	A94A
SetCCursor	AA1C	SetMenuFlash	
SetClientID	AA3C	SetMinCtl	A964
SetClip	A879	SetCtlMin	
SetCPixel	AA16	SetOrigin	A878
SetCPortPix	AA06	SetOSDefault	A083
SetCRefCon	A95B	SetPalette	AA95
SetCTitle	A95F	SetPBits	A875
SetCtlAction	A96B	SetPortBits	
SetCtlColor	AA43	SetPenState	A899
SetCtlValue	A963	SetPort	A873
SetCursor	A851	SetPt	A880
SetDateTime	A03A	SetPtrSize	A020
SetDefaultStartup	A07E	SetRecRgn	A8DE
SetDeskCPat	AA47	SetRectRgn	
SetDeviceAttribute	AA2D	SetRect	A8A7
SetDItem	A98E	SetResAttrs	A9A7
SetEmptyRgn	A8DD	SetResFileAttrs	A9F7
SetEntries	AA3F	SetResInfo	A9A9
SetEntryColor	AA9C	SetResLoad	A99B
SetEntryUsage	AA9E	SetResPurge	A993
SetEOF	A012	SetStdCProcs	AA4E
PBSetEOF		SetStdProcs	A8EA
SetFileInfo	A00D	SetString	A907
PBSetFInfo		SetTrapAddress	A047
SetFilLock	A041	SetVideoDefault	A081
PBSetFLock		SetVol	A015
SetFilType	A043	PBSetVol	
PBSetFVers		SetWinColor	AA41
SetFontLock	A903	SetWindowPic	A92E
SetFPos	A044	SetWRefCon	A918
PBSetFPos		SetWTitle	A91A
SetFScaleDisable	A834	SetZone	A01B
SetGDevice	AA31	ShieldCursor	A855
SetGrowZone	A04B	ShowControl	A957

Name	Trap word		Name	Trap word
ShowCursor	A853		sFindsInfoRecPtr	(47)
ShowDItem	A828		sFindsRsrcPtr	(48)
ShowHide	A908		sdeleteSRTRec	(49)
ShowPen	A897		SlotVInstall	A06F
ShowWindow	A915		SlotVRemove	A070
Shutdown	A895		SndAddModifier	A802
ShutDwnPower	(1)		SndControl	A806
ShutDwnStart	(2)		SndDisposeChannel	A801
ShutDwnInstall	(3)		SndDoCommand	A803
ShutDwnRemove	(4)		SndDoImmediate	A804
SIntInstall	A075		SndNewChannel	A807
SIntRemove	A076		SndPlay	A805
SizeControl	A95C		SpaceExtra	A88E
SizeRsrc	A9A5		StackSpace	A065
SizeResource			Status	A005
SizeWindow	A91D		PBStatus	
SlopeFromAngle	A8BC		StdArc	A8BD
SlotManager	A06E		StdBits	A8EB
sReadByte	(0)		StdComment	A8F1
sReadWord	(1)		StdGetPic	A8EE
sReadLong	(2)		StdLine	A890
sGetcString	(3)		StdOval	A8B6
sGetBlock	(5)		StdPoly	A8C5
sFindStruct	(6)		StdPutPic	A8F0
sReadStruct	(7)		StdRect	A8A0
sReadInfo	(16)		StdRgn	A8D1
sReadPRAMRec	(17)		StdRRect	A8AF
sPutPRAMRec	(18)		StdText	A882
sReadFHeader	(19)		StdTxMeas	A8ED
sNextRsrc	(20)		StillDown	A973
sNextTypesRsrc	(21)		StopAlert	A986
sRsrcInfo	(22)		StringWidth	A88C
sDisposePtr	(23)		StripAddress	A055
sCkCardStatus	(24)		StuffHex	A866
sReadDrvrName	(25)		SubPt	A87F
sFindDevBase	(27)		SwapMMUMode	A05D
InitSDeclMgr	(32)		SysBeep	A9C8
sPrimaryInit	(33)		SysEdit	A9C2
sCardChanged	(34)		SystemEdit	
sExec	(35)		SysEnvirons	A090
sOffsetData	(36)		SysError	A9C9
InitPRAMRecs	(37)		SystemClick	A9B3
sReadPBSize	(38)		SystemEvent	A9B2
sCalcStep	(40)		SystemMenu	A9B5
InitsRsrcTable	(41)		SystemTask	A9B4
sSearchSRT	(42)		TEActivate	A9D8
sUpdateSRT	(43)		TEAutoView	A813
sCalcsPointer	(44)		TECalText	A9D0
sGetDriver	(45)		TEClick	A9D4
sPtrToSlot	(46)		TECopy	A9D5

Name	Trap word	Name	Trap word
TECut	A9D6	TextMode	A889
TEDeactivate	A9D9	TextSize	A88A
TEDelete	A9D7	TextWidth	A886
TEDispatch	A83D	TickCount	A975
TEStylePaste	(0)	TrackBox	A83B
TESetStyle	(1)	TrackControl	A968
TEReplaceStyle	(2)	TrackGoAway	A91E
TEGetStyle	(3)	UnionRect	A8AB
GetStyleHandle	(4)	UnionRgn	A8E5
SetStyleHandle	(5)	Unique1ID	A810
GetStyleScrap	(6)	UniqueID	A9C1
TEStyleInsert	(7)	UnloadSeg	A9F1
TEGetPoint	(8)	UnlodeScrap	A9FA
TEGetHeight	(9)	UnloadScrap	
TEDispose	A9CD	UnmountVol	A00E
TEGetOffset	A83C	PBUnmountVol	
TEGetText	A9CB	UnpackBits	A8D0
TEIdle	A9DA	UpdateResFile	A999
TEInit	A9CC	UpdtControl	A953
TEInsert	A9DE	UpdtDialog	A978
TEKey	A9DC	UprString	A054
TENew	A9D2	UseResFile	A998
TEPaste	A9DB	ValidRect	A92A
TEPinScroll	A812	ValidRgn	A929
TEScroll	A9DD	VInstall	A033
TESelView	A811	VRemove	A034
TESetJust	A9DF	WaitMouseUp	A977
TESetSelect	A9D1	Write	A003
TESetText	A9CF	PBWrite	
TestControl	A966	WriteParam	A038
TestDeviceAttribute	AA2C	WriteResource	A9B0
TEStyleNew	A83E	X2Fix	A844
TEUpdate	A9D3	X2Frac	A846
TextBox	A9CE	XorRgn	A8E7
TextFace	A888	ZeroScrap	A9FC
TextFont	A887	ZoomWindow	A83A

Trap word	Name	Trap word	Name
A000	Open	A005	Status
	PBOpen		PBStatus
A001	Close	A006	KillIO
	PBClose		PBKillIO
A002	Read	A007	GetVolInfo
	PBRead		PBGetVInfo
A003	Write	A008	Create
	PBWrite		PBCreate
A004	Control	A009	Delete
	PBControl		PBDelete

Trap Word	Name	Trap Word	Name
A00A	OpenRF	A034	VRemove
	PBOpenRF	A035	Offline
A00B	Rename		PBOffline
	PBRename	A036	MoreMasters
A00C	GetFileInfo	A038	WriteParam
	PBGetInfo	A039	ReadDateTime
A00D	SetFileInfo	A03A	SetDateTime
	PBSetFInfo	A03B	Delay
A00E	UnmountVol	A03C	CmpString
	PBUnmountVol		EqualString
A00F	MountVol	A03D	DrvrInstall
	PBMountVol		(internal use only)
A010	Allocate	A03E	DrvrRemove
	PBAllocate		(internal use only)
A011	GetEOF	A03F	InitUtil
	PBGetEOF	A040	ResrvMem
A012	SetEOF	A041	SetFilLock
	PBSetEOF		PBSetFLock
A013	FlushVol	A042	RstFilLock
	PBFlushVol		PBRstFLock
A014	GetVol	A043	SetFilType
	PBGetVol		PBSetFVers
A015	SetVol	A044	SetFPos
	PBSetVol		PBSetFPos
A016	InitQueue	A045	FlushFile
A017	Eject		PBFlushFile
	PBEject	A047	SetTrapAddress
A018	GetFPos	A049	HPurge
	PBGetFPos	A04A	HNoPurge
A019	InitZone	A04B	SetGrowZone
A01B	SetZone	A04C	CompactMem
A01C	FreeMem	A04D	PurgeMem
A01F	DisposPtr	A04E	AddDrive
A020	SetPtrSize		(internal use only)
A021	GetPtrSize	A04F	RDrvrInstall
A023	DisposHandle		(internal use only)
A024	SetHandleSize	A050	RelString
A025	GetHandleSize	A054	UprString
A027	ReallocHandle	A055	StripAddress
A029	HLock	A057	SetAppBase
A02A	HUnlock		SetApplBase
A02B	EmptyHandle	A05D	SwapMMUMode
A02C	InitApplZone	A061	MaxBlock
A02D	SetApplLimit	A062	PurgeSpace
A02E	BlockMove	A063	MaxApplZone
A02F	PostEvent	A064	MoveHHi
A030	OSEventAvail	A065	StackSpace
A031	GetOSEvent	A066	NewEmptyHandle
A032	FlushEvents	A067	HSetRBit
A033	VInstall	A068	HClrRBit

Trap Word	Name		Trap Word	Name	
A069	HGetState		A07E	SetDefaultStartup	
A06A	HSetState		A07F	InternalWait	
A06E	SlotManager			SetTimeout	(0)
	sReadByte	(0)		GetTimeout	(1)
	sReadWord	(1)	A080	GetVideoDefault	
	sReadLong	(2)	A081	SetVideoDefault	
	sGetcString	(3)	A082	SIntInstall	
	sGetBlock	(5)	A083	SetOSDefault	
	sFindStruct	(6)	A084	GetOSDefault	
	sReadStruct	(7)	A090	SysEnvirons	
	sReadInfo	(16)	A11A	GetZone	
	sReadPRAMRec	(17)	A11D	MaxMem	
	sPutPRAMRec	(18)	A11E	NewPtr	
	sReadFHeader	(19)	A122	NewHandle	
	sNextRsrc	(20)	A126	HandleZone	
	sNextTypesRsrc	(21)	A128	RecoverHandle	
	sRsrcInfo	(22)	A12F	PPostEvent	
	sDisposePtr	(23)	A146	GetTrapAddress	
	sCkCardStatus	(24)	A148	PtrZone	
	sReadDrvrName	(25)	A260	HFSDispatch	
	sFindDevBase	(27)		OpenWD	(1)
	sPrimaryInit	(33)		CloseWD	(2)
	sCardChanged	(34)		CatMove	(5)
	sExec	(35)		DirCreate	(6)
	sOffsetData	(36)		GetWDInfo	(7)
	InitPRAMRecs	(37)		GetFCBInfo	(8)
	sReadPBSize	(38)		GetCatInfo	(9)
	sCalcStep	(40)		SetCatInfo	(10)
	InitsRsrcTable	(41)		SetVolInfo	(11)
	sSearchSRT	(42)		LockRng	(16)
	sUpdateSRT	(43)		UnlockRng	(17)
	sCalcsPointer	(44)	A801	SndDisposeChannel	
	sGetDriver	(45)	A802	SndAddModifier	
	sPtrToSlot	(46)	A803	SndDoCommand	
	sFindsInfoRecPtr	(47)	A804	SndDoImmediate	
	sFindsRsrcPtr	(48)	A805	SndPlay	
	sdeleteSRTRec	(49)	A806	SndControl	
A06F	SlotVInstall		A807	SndNewChannel	
A070	SlotVRemove		A808	InitProcMenu	
A071	AttachVBL		A809	GetCVariant	
A072	DoVBLTask		A80A	GetWVariant	
A075	DTInstall		A80B	PopUpMenuSelect	
A076	SIntRemove		A80C	RGetResource	
A077	CountADBs		A80D	Count1Resources	
A078	GetIndADB		A80E	Get1IxResource	
A079	GetADBInfo			Get1IndResource	
A07A	SetADBInfo		A80F	Get1IxType	
A07B	ADBReInit			Get1IndType	
A07C	ADBOp		A810	Unique1ID	
A07D	GetDefaultStartup		A811	TESelView	

Trap Word	Name			Trap Word	Name		
A812	TEPinScroll			A83B	TrackBox		
A813	TEAutoView			A83C	TEGetOffset		
A815	SCSIDispatch			A83D	TEDispatch		
	SCSIReset	(0)			TEStylePaste	(0)	
	SCSIGet	(1)			TESetStyle	(1)	
	SCSISelect	(2)			TEReplaceStyle	(2)	
	SCSICmd	(3)			TEGetStyle	(3)	
	SCSIComplete	(4)			GetStyleHandle	(4)	
	SCSIRead	(5)			SetStyleHandle	(5)	
	SCSIWrite	(6)			GetStyleScrap	(6)	
	SCSIInstall	(7)			TEStyleInsert	(7)	
	SCSIRBlind	(8)			TEGetPoint	(8)	
	SCSIWBlind	(9)			TEGetHeight	(9)	
	SCSIStat	(10)		A83E	TEStyleNew		
	SCSISelAtn	(11)		A83F	Long2Fix		
	SCSIMsgIn	(12)		A840	Fix2Long		
	SCSIMsgOut	(13)		A841	Fix2Frac		
A816	Pack8			A842	Frac2Fix		
A817	CopyMask			A843	Fix2X		
A818	FixAtan2			A844	X2Fix		
A81C	Count1Types			A845	Frac2X		
A81F	Get1Resource			A846	X2Frac		
A820	Get1NamedResource			A847	FracCos		
A821	MaxSizeRsrc			A848	FracSin		
A826	InsMenuItem			A849	FracSqrt		
A827	HideDItem			A84A	FracMul		
A828	ShowDItem			A84B	FracDiv		
A82B	Pack9			A84D	FixDiv		
A82C	Pack10			A84E	GetItemCmd		
A82D	Pack11			A84F	SetItemCmd		
A82E	Pack12			A850	InitCursor		
	Fix2SmallFract	(1)		A851	SetCursor		
	SmallFract2Fix	(2)		A852	HideCursor		
	CMY2RGB	(3)		A853	ShowCursor		
	RGB2CMY	(4)		A855	ShieldCursor		
	HSL2RGB	(5)		A856	ObscureCursor		
	RGB2HSL	(6)		A858	BitAnd		
	HSV2RGB	(7)		A859	BitXor		
	RGB2HSV	(8)		A85A	BitNot		
	GetColor	(9)		A85B	BitOr		
A82F	Pack13			A85C	BitShift		
A830	Pack14			A85D	BitTst		
A831	Pack15			A85E	BitSet		
A834	SetFScaleDisable			A85F	BitClr		
A835	FontMetrics			A861	Random		
A836	GetMaskTable			A862	ForeColor		
A837	MeasureText			A863	BackColor		
A838	CalcMask			A864	ColorBit		
A839	SeedFill			A865	GetPixel		
A83A	ZoomWindow			A866	StuffHex		

Trap Word	Name		Trap Word	Name	
A867	LongMul			ShutDwnInstall	(3)
A868	FixMul			ShutDwnRemove	(4)
A869	FixRatio		A896	HidePen	
A86A	HiWord		A897	ShowPen	
A86B	LoWord		A898	GetPenState	
A86C	FixRound		A899	SetPenState	
A86D	InitPort		A89A	GetPen	
A86E	InitGraf		A89B	PenSize	
A86F	OpenPort		A89C	PenMode	
A870	LocalToGlobal		A89D	PenPat	
A871	GlobalToLocal		A89E	PenNormal	
A872	GrafDevice		A8A0	StdRect	
A873	SetPort		A8A1	FrameRect	
A874	GetPort		A8A2	PaintRect	
A875	SetPBits		A8A3	EraseRect	
	SetPortBits		A8A4	InverRect	
A876	PortSize			InvertRect	
A877	MovePortTo		A8A5	FillRect	
A878	SetOrigin		A8A6	EqualRect	
A879	SetClip		A8A7	SetRect	
A87A	GetClip		A8A8	OffsetRect	
A87B	ClipRect		A8A9	InsetRect	
A87C	BackPat		A8AA	SectRect	
A87D	CloseCPort		A8AB	UnionRect	
A87D	ClosePort		A8AC	Pt2Rect	
A87E	AddPt		A8AD	PtInRect	
A87F	SubPt		A8AE	EmptyRect	
A880	SetPt		A8AF	StdRRect	
A881	EqualPt		A8B0	FrameRoundRect	
A882	StdText		A8B1	PaintRoundRect	
A883	DrawChar		A8B2	EraseRoundRect	
A884	DrawString		A8B3	InverRoundRect	
A885	DrawText			InvertRoundRect	
A886	TextWidth		A8B4	FillRoundRect	
A887	TextFont		A8B5	ScriptUtil	
A888	TextFace			smFontScript	(0)
A889	TextMode			smIntlScript	(2)
A88A	TextSize			smKybdScript	(4)
A88B	GetFontInfo			smFont2Script	(6)
A88C	StringWidth			smGetEnvirons	(8)
A88D	CharWidth			smSetEnvirons	(10)
A88E	SpaceExtra			smGetScript	(12)
A890	StdLine			smSetScript	(14)
A891	LineTo			smCharByte	(16)
A892	Line			smCharType	(18)
A893	MoveTo			smPixel2Char	(20)
A894	Move			smChar2Pixel	(22)
A895	Shutdown			smTranslit	(24)
	ShutDwnPower	(1)		smFindWord	(26)
	ShutDwnStart	(2)		smHiliteText	(28)

Trap Word	Name		Trap Word	Name
	smDrawJust	(30)	A8E2	EmptyRgn
	smMeasureJust	(32)	A8E3	EqualRgn
A8B6	StdOval		A8E4	SectRgn
A8B7	FrameOval		A8E5	UnionRgn
A8B8	PaintOval		A8E6	DiffRgn
A8B9	EraseOval		A8E7	XorRgn
A8BA	InvertOval		A8E8	PtInRgn
A8BB	FillOval		A8E9	RectInRgn
A8BC	SlopeFromAngle		A8EA	SetStdProcs
A8BD	StdArc		A8EB	StdBits
A8BE	FrameArc		A8EC	CopyBits
A8BF	PaintArc		A8ED	StdTxMeas
A8C0	EraseArc		A8EE	StdGetPic
A8C1	InvertArc		A8EF	ScrollRect
A8C2	FillArc		A8F0	StdPutPic
A8C3	PtToAngle		A8F1	StdComment
A8C4	AngleFromSlope		A8F2	PicComment
A8C5	StdPoly		A8F3	OpenPicture
A8C6	FramePoly		A8F4	ClosePicture
A8C7	PaintPoly		A8F5	KillPicture
A8C8	ErasePoly		A8F6	DrawPicture
A8C9	InvertPoly		A8F8	ScalePt
A8CA	FillPoly		A8F9	MapPt
A8CB	OpenPoly		A8FA	MapRect
A8CC	ClosePgon		A8FB	MapRgn
	ClosePoly		A8FC	MapPoly
A8CD	KillPoly		A8FD	PrGlue
A8CE	OffsetPoly		A8FE	InitFonts
A8CF	PackBits		A8FF	GetFName
A8D0	UnpackBits			GetFontName
A8D1	StdRgn		A900	GetFNum
A8D2	FrameRgn		A901	FMSwapFont
A8D3	PaintRgn		A902	RealFont
A8D4	EraseRgn		A903	SetFontLock
A8D5	InverRgn		A904	DrawGrowIcon
	InvertRgn		A905	DragGrayRgn
A8D6	FillRgn		A906	NewString
A8D8	NewRgn		A907	SetString
A8D9	DisposRgn		A908	ShowHide
	DisposeRgn		A909	CalcVis
A8DA	OpenRgn		A90A	CalcVBehind
A8DB	CloseRgn			CalcVisBehind
A8DC	CopyRgn		A90B	ClipAbove
A8DD	SetEmptyRgn		A90C	PaintOne
A8DE	SetRecRgn		A90D	PaintBehind
A8DF	SetRectRgn		A90E	SaveOld
	RectRgn		A90F	DrawNew
A8E0	OfsetRgn		A910	GetWMgrPort
	OffsetRgn		A911	CheckUpdate
A8E1	InsetRgn		A912	InitWindows

Trap Word	Name	Trap Word	Name
A913	NewWindow	A941	GetItmStyle
A914	DisposWindow		GetItemStyle
	DisposeWindow	A942	SetItmStyle
A915	ShowWindow		SetItemStyle
A916	HideWindow	A943	GetItmMark
A917	GetWRefCon		GetItemMark
A918	SetWRefCon	A944	SetItmMark
A919	GetWTitle		SetItemMark
A91A	SetWTitle	A945	CheckItem
A91B	MoveWindow	A946	GetItem
A91C	HiliteWindow	A947	SetItem
A91D	SizeWindow	A948	CalcMenuSize
A91E	TrackGoAway	A949	GetMHandle
A91F	SelectWindow	A94A	SetMFlash
A920	BringToFront		SetMenuFlash
A921	SendBehind	A94B	PlotIcon
A922	BeginUpdate	A94C	FlashMenuBar
A923	EndUpdate	A94D	AddResMenu
A924	FrontWindow	A94E	PinRect
A925	DragWindow	A94F	DeltaPoint
A926	DragTheRgn	A950	CountMItems
A927	InvalRgn	A951	InsertResMenu
A928	InvalRect	A952	DelMenuItem
A929	ValidRgn	A953	UpdtControl
A92A	ValidRect	A954	NewControl
A92B	GrowWindow	A955	DisposControl
A92C	FindWindow		DisposeControl
A92D	CloseWindow	A956	KillControls
A92E	SetWindowPic	A957	ShowControl
A92F	GetWindowPic	A958	HideControl
A930	InitMenus	A959	MoveControl
A931	NewMenu	A95A	GetCRefCon
A932	DisposMenu	A95B	SetCRefCon
	DisposeMenu	A95C	SizeControl
A933	AppendMenu	A95D	HiliteControl
A934	ClearMenuBar	A95E	GetCTitle
A935	InsertMenu	A95F	SetCTitle
A936	DeleteMenu	A960	GetCtlValue
A937	DrawMenuBar	A961	GetMinCtl
A938	HiliteMenu		GetCtlMin
A939	EnableItem	A962	GetMaxCtl
A93A	DisableItem		GetCtlMax
A93B	GetMenuBar	A963	SetCtlValue
A93C	SetMenuBar	A964	SetMinCtl
A93D	MenuSelect		SetCtlMin
A93E	MenuKey	A965	SetMaxCtl
A93F	GetItmIcon		SetCtlMax
	GetItemIcon	A966	TestControl
A940	SetItmIcon	A967	DragControl
	SetItemIcon	A968	TrackControl

Trap Word	Name	Trap Word	Name
A969	DrawControls	A99B	SetResLoad
A96A	GetCtlAction	A99C	CountResources
A96B	SetCtlAction	A99D	GetIndResource
A96C	FindControl	A99E	CountTypes
A96D	Draw1Control	A99F	GetIndType
A96E	Dequeue	A9A0	GetResource
A96F	Enqueue	A9A1	GetNamedResource
A970	GetNextEvent	A9A2	LoadResource
A971	EventAvail	A9A3	ReleaseResource
A972	GetMouse	A9A4	HomeResFile
A973	StillDown	A9A5	SizeRsrc
A974	Button		SizeResource
A975	TickCount	A9A6	GetResAttrs
A976	GetKeys	A9A7	SetResAttrs
A977	WaitMouseUp	A9A8	GetResInfo
A978	UpdtDialog	A9A9	SetResInfo
A979	CouldDialog	A9AA	ChangedResource
A97A	FreeDialog	A9AB	AddResource
A97B	InitDialogs	A9AD	RmveResource
A97C	GetNewDialog	A9AF	ResError
A97D	NewDialog	A9B0	WriteResource
A97E	SelIText	A9B1	CreateResFile
A97F	IsDialogEvent	A9B2	SystemEvent
A980	DialogSelect	A9B3	SystemClick
A981	DrawDialog	A9B4	SystemTask
A982	CloseDialog	A9B5	SystemMenu
A983	DisposDialog	A9B6	OpenDeskAcc
A984	FindDItem	A9B7	CloseDeskAcc
A985	Alert	A9B8	GetPattern
A986	StopAlert	A9B9	GetCursor
A987	NoteAlert	A9BA	GetString
A988	CautionAlert	A9BB	GetIcon
A989	CouldAlert	A9BC	GetPicture
A98A	FreeAlert	A9BD	GetNewWindow
A98B	ParamText	A9BE	GetNewControl
A98C	ErrorSound	A9BF	GetRMenu
A98D	GetDItem		GetMenu
A98E	SetDItem	A9C0	GetNewMBar
A98F	SetIText	A9C1	UniqueID
A990	GetIText	A9C2	SysEdit
A991	ModalDialog		SystemEdit
A992	DetachResource	A9C3	KeyTrans
A993	SetResPurge	A9C4	OpenRFPerm
A994	CurResFile	A9C5	RsrcMapEntry
A995	InitResources	A9C6	Secs2Date
A996	RsrcZoneInit	A9C7	Date2Secs
A997	OpenResFile	A9C8	SysBeep
A998	UseResFile	A9C9	SysError
A999	UpdateResFile	A9CB	TEGetText
A99A	CloseResFile	A9CC	TEInit

Trap Word	Name		Trap Word	Name	
A9CD	TEDispose			LSetSelect	(92)
A9CE	TextBox			LSize	(96)
A9CF	TESetText			LUpdate	(100)
A9D0	TECalText		A9E8	Pack1	
A9D1	TESetSelect			(reserved for future use)	
A9D2	TENew		A9E9	Pack2	
A9D3	TEUpdate			DIBadMount	(0)
A9D4	TEClick			DILoad	(2)
A9D5	TECopy			DIUnload	(4)
A9D6	TECut			DIFormat	(6)
A9D7	TEDelete			DIVerify	(8)
A9D8	TEActivate			DIZero	(10)
A9D9	TEDeactivate		A9EA	Pack3	
A9DA	TEIdle			SFPutFile	(1)
A9DB	TEPaste			SFGetFile	(2)
A9DC	TEKey			SFPPutFile	(3)
A9DD	TEScroll			SFPGetFile	(4)
A9DE	TEInsert		A9EB	Pack4	
A9DF	TESetJust			(synonym: FP68K)	
A9E0	Munger		A9EC	Pack5	
A9E1	HandToHand			(synonym: Elems68K)	
A9E2	PtrToXHand		A9ED	Pack6	
A9E3	PtrToHand			IUDateString	(0)
A9E4	HandAndHand			IUTimeString	(2)
A9E5	InitPack			IUMetric	(4)
A9E6	InitAllPacks			IUDGetIntl	(6)
A9E7	Pack0			IUSetIntl	(8)
	LActivate	(0)		IUMagString	(10)
	LAddColumn	(4)		IUMagIDString	(12)
	LAddRow	(8)		IUDatePString	(14)
	LAddToCell	(12)		IUTimePString	(16)
	LAutoScroll	(16)	A9EE	Pack7	
	LCellSize	(20)		NumToString	(0)
	LClick	(24)		StringToNum	(1)
	LClrCell	(28)		PStr2Dec	(2)
	LDelColumn	(32)		CStr2Dec	(4)
	LDelRow	(36)	A9EF	PtrAndHand	
	LDispose	(40)	A9F0	LoadSeg	
	LDoDraw	(44)	A9F1	UnloadSeg	
	LDraw	(48)	A9F2	Launch	
	LFind	(52)	A9F3	Chain	
	LGetCell	(56)	A9F4	ExitToShell	
	LGetSelect	(60)	A9F5	GetAppParms	
	LLastClick	(64)	A9F6	GetResFileAttrs	
	LNew	(68)	A9F7	SetResFileAttrs	
	LNextCell	(72)	A9F9	InfoScrap	
	LRect	(76)	A9FA	UnlodeScrap	
	LScroll	(80)		UnloadScrap	
	LSearch	(84)	A9FB	LodeScrap	
	LSetCell	(88)		LoadScrap	

Trap Word	Name	Trap Word	Name
A9FC	ZeroScrap	AA31	SetGDevice
A9FD	GetScrap	AA32	GetGDevice
A9FE	PutScrap	AA33	Color2Index
AA00	OpenCport	AA34	Index2Color
AA01	InitCport	AA35	InvertColor
AA03	NewPixMap	AA36	RealColor
AA04	DisposPixMap	AA37	GetSubTable
AA05	CopyPixMap	AA39	MakeITable
AA06	SetCPortPix	AA3A	AddSearch
AA07	NewPixPat	AA3B	AddComp
AA08	DisposPixPat	AA3C	SetClientID
AA09	CopyPixPat	AA3D	ProtectEntry
AA0A	PenPixPat	AA3E	ReserveEntry
AA0B	BackPixPat	AA3F	SetEntries
AA0C	GetPixPat	AA40	QDError
AA0D	MakeRGBPat	AA41	SetWinColor
AA0E	FillCRect	AA42	GetAuxWin
AA0F	FillCOval	AA43	SetCtlColor
AA10	FillCRoundRect	AA44	GetAuxCtl
AA11	FillCArc	AA45	NewCWindow
AA12	FillCRgn	AA46	GetNewCWindow
AA13	FillCPoly	AA47	SetDeskCPat
AA14	RGBForeColor	AA48	GetCWMgrPort
AA15	RGBBackColor	AA49	SaveEntries
AA16	SetCPixel	AA4A	RestoreEntries
AA17	GetCPixel	AA4B	NewCDialog
AA18	GetCTable	AA4C	DelSearch
AA19	GetForeColor	AA4D	DelComp
AA1A	GetBackColor	AA4E	SetStdCProcs
AA1B	GetCCursor	AA4F	CalcCMask
AA1C	SetCCursor	AA50	SeedCFill
AA1D	AllocCursor	AA60	DelMCEntries
AA1E	GetCIcon	AA61	GetMCInfo
AA1F	PlotCIcon	AA62	SetMCInfo
AA21	OpColor	AA63	DispMCInfo
AA22	HiliteColor	AA64	GetMCEntry
AA23	CharExtra	AA65	SetMCEntries
AA24	DisposCTable	AA66	MenuChoice
AA25	DisposCIcon	AA90	InitPalettes
AA26	DisposCCursor	AA91	NewPalette
AA27	GetMaxDevice	AA92	GetNewPalette
AA28	GetCTSeed	AA93	DisposePalette
AA29	GetDeviceList	AA94	ActivatePalette
AA2A	GetMainDevice	AA95	SetPalette
AA2B	GetNextDevice	AA96	GetPalette
AA2C	TestDeviceAttribute	AA97	PmForeColor
AA2D	SetDeviceAttribute	AA98	PmBackColor
AA2E	InitGDevice	AA99	AnimateEntry
AA2F	NewGDevice	AA9A	AnimatePalette
AA30	DisposGDevice	AA9B	GetEntryColor

Trap Word	Name
AA9C	SetEntryColor
AA9D	GetEntryUsage
AA9E	SetEntryUsage
AA9F	CTab2Palette
AAA0	Palette2CTab

APPENDIX C: GLOBAL VARIABLES

This appendix gives an alphabetical list of all system global variables described in *Inside Macintosh*, along with their locations in memory.

Name	Location	Contents
ABusVars	$2D8	Pointer to AppleTalk variables
ACount	$A9A	Stage number (0 through 3) of last alert (word)
ANumber	$A98	Resource ID of last alert (word)
ApFontID	$984	Font number of application font (word)
ApplLimit	$130	Application heap limit
ApplScratch	$A78	12-byte scratch area reserved for use by applications
ApplZone	$2AA	Address of application heap zone
AppParmHandle	$AEC	Handle to Finder information
AtMenuBottom	$A0C	Flag for menu scrolling (word)
AuxWinHead	$CD0	Auxiliary window list header (long)
BootDrive	$210	Working directory reference number for system startup volume (word)
BufPtr	$10C	Address of end of jump table
BufTgDate	$304	File tags buffer: date and time of last modification (long)
BufTgFBkNum	$302	File tags buffer: logical block number (word)
BufTgFFlg	$300	File tags buffer: flags (word: bit 1=1 if resource fork)
BufTgFNum	$2FC	File tags buffer: file number (long)
CaretTime	$2F4	Caret-blink interval in ticks (long)
CPUFlag	$12F	Microprocessor in use (word)
CrsrThresh	$8EC	Mouse-scaling threshold (word)
CurActivate	$A64	Pointer to window to receive activate event
CurApName	$910	Name of current application (length byte followed by up to 31 characters)
CurApRefNum	$900	Reference number of current application's resource file (word)
CurDeactive	$A68	Pointer to window to receive deactivate event
CurDirStore	$398	Directory ID of directory last opened (long)
CurJTOffset	$934	Offset to jump table from location pointed to by A5 (word)
CurMap	$A5A	Reference number of current resource file (word)
CurPageOption	$936	Sound/screen buffer configuration passed to Chain or Launch (word)

Name	Location	Contents
CurPitch	$280	Value of count in square-wave synthesizer buffer (word)
CurrentA5	$904	Address of boundary between application globals and application parameters
CurStackBase	$908	Address of base of stack; start of application globals
DABeeper	$A9C	Address of current sound procedure
DAStrings	$AA0	Handles to ParamText strings (16 bytes)
DefltStack	$322	Default space allotment for stack (long)
DefVCBPtr	$352	Pointer to default volume control block
DeskHook	$A6C	Address of procedure for painting desktop or responding to clicks on desktop
DeskPattern	$A3C	Pattern with which desktop is painted (8 bytes)
DeviceList	$8A8	Handle to the first element in the device list
DlgFont	$AFA	Font number for dialogs and alerts (word)
DoubleTime	$2F0	Double-click interval in ticks (long)
DragHook	$9F6	Address of procedure to execute during TrackGoAway, DragWindow, GrowWindow, DragGrayRgn, TrackControl, and DragControl
DragPattern	$A34	Pattern of dragged region's outline (8 bytes)
DrvQHdr	$308	Drive queue header (10 bytes)
DSAlertRect	$3F8	Rectangle enclosing system error alert (8 bytes)
DSAlertTab	$2BA	Pointer to system error alert table in use
DSErrCode	$AF0	Current system error ID (word)
DTQueue	$D92	Deferred task queue header (10 bytes)
EventQueue	$14A	Event queue header (10 bytes)
ExtStsDT	$2BE	External/status interrupt vector table (16 bytes)
FCBSPtr	$34E	Pointer to file-control-block buffer
FinderName	$2E0	Name of the Finder (length byte followed by up to 15 characters)
FractEnable	$BF4	Nonzero to enable fractional widths (byte)
FScaleDisable	$A63	Nonzero to disable font scaling (byte)
FSFCBLen	$3F6	Size of a file control block; on 64K ROM, it contains –1 (word)
FSQHdr	$360	File I/O queue header (10 bytes)
GhostWindow	$A84	Pointer to window never to be considered frontmost
GrayRgn	$9EE	Handle to region drawn as desktop
GZRootHnd	$328	Handle to relocatable block not to be moved by grow zone function

Name	Location	Contents
HeapEnd	$114	Address of end of application heap zone
HiliteMode	$938	Set if highlighting is on
HiliteRGB	$DA0	Default highlight color for the system
IntlSpec	$BA0	International software installed if not equal to −1 (long)
JADBProc	06B8	Pointer to ADBReInit preprocessing/ postprocessing routine
JDTInstall	$D9C	Jump vector for DTInstall routine
JFetch	$8F4	Jump vector for Fetch function
JIODone	$8FC	Jump vector for IODone function
JournalRef	$8E8	Reference number of journaling device driver (word)
JStash	$8F8	Jump vector for Stash function
JVBLTask	$D28	Jump vector for DoVBLTask routine
KbdLast	$218	ADB address of the keyboard last used (byte)
KbdType	$21E	Keyboard type of the keyboard last used (byte)
KeyRepThresh	$190	Auto-key rate (word)
KeyThresh	$18E	Auto-key threshold (word)
LastFOND	$BC2	Handle to last family record used
Lo3Bytes	$31A	$00FFFFFF
Lvl2DT	$1B2	Level-2 secondary interrupt vector table (32 bytes)
MainDevice	$8A4	Handle to the current main device
MBarEnable	$A20	Unique menu ID for active desk accessory, when menu bar belongs to the accessory (word)
MBarHeight	$BAA	Height of menu bar (word)
MBarHook	$A2C	Address of routine called by MenuSelect before menu is drawn
MemErr	$220	Current value of MemError (word)
MemTop	$108	Address of end of RAM (on Macintosh XL, end of RAM available to applications)
MenuCInfo	$D50	Header for menu color information table
MenuDisable	$B54	Menu ID and item for slected diasabled item
MenuFlash	$A24	Count for duration of menu item blinking (word)
MenuHook	$A30	Address of routine called during MenuSelect
MenuList	$A1C	Handle to current menu list
MinStack	$31E	Minimum space allotment for stack (long)
MinusOne	$A06	$FFFFFFFF
MMU32Bit	$CB2	Current address mode (byte)

Name	Location	Contents
OldContent	$9EA	Handle to saved content region
OldStructure	$9E6	Handle to saved structure region
OneOne	$A02	$00010001
PaintWhite	$9DC	Flag for whether to paint window white before update event (word)
PortBUse	$291	Current availability of serial port B (byte)
PrintErr	$944	Result code from last Printing Manager routine (word)
QDColors	$8B0	Default QuickDraw colors
RAMBase	$2B2	Trap dispatch table's base address for routines in RAM
ResErr	$A60	Current value of ResError (word)
ResErrProc	$AF2	Address of resource error procedure
ResLoad	$A5E	Current SetResLoad state (word)
ResumeProc	$A8C	Address of resume procedure
RndSeed	$156	Random number seed (long)
ROM85	$28E	Version number of ROM (word)
ROMBase	$2AE	Base address of ROM
ROMBase	$2AE	Base address of ROM
ROMFont0	$980	Handle to font record for system font
RomMapInsert	$B9E	Flag for whether to insert map to the ROM resources (byte)
SaveUpdate	$9DA	Flag for whether to generate update events (word)
SaveVisRgn	$9F2	Handle to saved visRgn
SCCRd	$1D8	SCC read base address
SCCWr	$1DC	SCC write base address
ScrapCount	$968	Count changed by ZeroScrap (word)
ScrapHandle	$964	Handle to desk scrap in memory
ScrapName	$96C	Pointer to scrap file name (preceded by length byte)
ScrapSize	$960	Size in bytes of desk scrap (long)
ScrapState	$96A	Tells where desk scrap is (word)
Scratch8	$9FA	8-byte scratch area
Scratch20	$1E4	20-byte scratch area
ScrDmpEnb	$2F8	0 if GetNextEvent shouldn't process Command-Shift-number combinations (byte)
ScrHRes	$104	Pixels per inch horizontally (word)
ScrnBase	$824	Address of main screen buffer

Name	Location	Contents
ScrVRes	$102	Pixels per inch vertically (word)
SdVolume	$260	Current speaker volume (byte: low-order three bits only)
SEvtEnb	$15C	0 if SystemEvent should return FALSE (byte)
SFSaveDisk	$214	Negative of volume reference number, used by Standard File Package (word)
SoundBase	$266	Pointer to free-form synthesizer buffer
SoundLevel	$27F	Amplitude in 740-byte buffer (byte)
SoundPtr	$262	Pointer to four-tone record
SPAlarm	$200	Alarm setting (long)
SPATalkA	$1F9	AppleTalk node ID hint for modem port (byte)
SPATalkB	$1FA	AppleTalk node ID hint for printer port (byte)
SPClikCaret	$209	Double-click and caret-blink times (byte)
SPConfig	$1FB	Use types for serial ports (byte)
SPFont	$204	Application font number minus 1 (word)
SPKbd	$206	Auto-key threshold and rate (byte)
SPMisc2	$20B	Mouse scaling, system startup disk, menu blink (byte)
SPPortA	$1FC	Modem port configuration (word)
SPPortB	$1FE	Printer port configuration (word)
SPPrint	$207	Printer connection (byte)
SPValid	$1F8	Validity status (byte)
SPVolCtl	$208	Speaker volume setting in parameter RAM (byte)
SynListHandle	$D32	Handle to synthetic font list
SysEvtMask	$144	System event mask (word)
SysFontFam	$BA6	If nonzero, the font number to use for system font (word)
SysFontSize	$BA8	If nonzero, the size of the system font (word)
SysMap	$A58	Reference number of system resource file (word)
SysMapHndl	$A54	Handle to map of system resource file
SysParam	$1F8	Low-memory copy of parameter RAM (20 bytes)
SysResName	$AD8	Name of system resource file (length byte followed by up to 19 characters)
SysZone	$2A6	Address of system heap zone
TEDoText	$A70	Address of TextEdit multi-purpose routine
TERecal	$A74	Address of routine to recalculate line starts for TextEdit
TEScrpHandle	$AB4	Handle to TextEdit scrap

Name	Location	Contents
TEScrpLength	$AB0	Size in bytes of TextEdit scrap (long)
TheGDevice	$CC8	Handle to current active device (long)
TheMenu	$A26	Menu ID of currently highlighted menu (word)
TheZone	$118	Address of current heap zone
Ticks	$16A	Current number of ticks since system startup (long)
Time	$20C	Seconds since midnight, January 1, 1904 (long)
TimeDBRA	$D00	Number of times the DBRA instruction can be executed per millisecond (word)
TimeSCCDB	$D02	Number of times the SCC can be accessed per millisecond (word)
TimeSCSIDB	$DA6	Number of times the SCSI can be accessed per millisecond (word)
TmpResLoad	$B9F	Temporary SetResLoad state for calls using ROMMapInsert (byte)
ToExtFS	$3F2	Pointer to external file system
ToolScratch	$9CE	8-byte scratch area
TopMapHndl	$A50	Handle to resource map of most recently opened resource file
TopMenuItem	$A0A	Pixel value of top of scrollable menu
UTableBase	$11C	Base address of unit table
VBLQueue	$160	Vertical retrace queue header (10 bytes)
VCBQHdr	$356	Volume-control-block queue header (10 bytes)
VIA	$1DA	VIA base address
WidthListHand	$8E4	Handle to a list of handles to recently-used width tables
WidthPtr	$B10	Pointer to global width table
WidthTabHandle	$B2A	Handle to global width table
WindowList	$9D6	Pointer to first window in window list; 0 if using events but not windows
WMgrPort	$9DE	Pointer to Window Manager port

GLOSSARY

access path: A description of the route that the File Manager follows to access a file; created when a file is opened.

access path buffer: Memory used by the File Manager to transfer data between an application and a file.

acknowledge cycle: For the NuBus: Last period of a transaction during which /ACK is asserted by a slave responding to a master. Often shortened to *ack cycle*.

action procedure: A procedure, used by the Control Manager function TrackControl, that defines an action to be performed repeatedly for as long as the mouse button is held down.

activate event: An event generated by the Window Manager when a window changes from active to inactive or vice versa.

active control: A control that will respond to the user's actions with the mouse.

active end: In a selection, the location to which the insertion point moves to complete the selection.

active window: The frontmost window on the desktop.

ADB device table: A structure in the system heap that lists all devices connected to the Apple DeskTop Bus.

address: A number used to identify a location in the computer's address space. Some locations are allocated to memory, others to I/O devices.

address mark: In a sector, information that's used internally by the Disk Driver, including information it uses to determine the position of the sector on the disk.

ALAP: See **AppleTalk Link Access Protocol.**

ALAP frame: A packet of data transmitted and received by ALAP.

ALAP protocol type: An identifier used to match particular kinds of packets with a particular protocol handler.

alert: A warning or report of an error, in the form of an alert box, sound from the Macintosh's speaker, or both.

alert box: A box that appears on the screen to give a warning or report an error during a Macintosh application.

alert template: A resource that contains information from which the Dialog Manager can create an alert.

alert window: The window in which an alert box is displayed.

alias: A different name for the same entity.

allocate: To reserve an area of memory for use.

allocation block: Volume space composed of an integral number of logical blocks.

amplitude: The maximum vertical distance of a periodic wave from the horizontal line about which the wave oscillates.

AMU (Address Mapping Unit): For the Macintosh II: A custom integrated circuit that allows an operating system to quickly reconfigure the arrangement of memory without physically moving data. Different tasks can be "swapped" within the same space.

anchor point: In a selection, the location of the insertion point when the selection was started.

AppleTalk address: A socket's number and its node ID number.

AppleTalk Link Access Protocol (ALAP): The lowest-level protocol in the AppleTalk architecture, managing node-to-node delivery of frames on a single AppleTalk network.

AppleTalk Manager: An interface to a pair of RAM device drivers that enable programs to send and receive information via an AppleTalk network.

AppleTalk Transaction Protocol (ATP): An AppleTalk protocol that's a DDP client. It allows one ATP client to request another ATP client to perform some activity and report the activity's result as a response to the requesting socket with guaranteed delivery.

application font: The font your application will use unless you specify otherwise—Geneva, by default.

application heap: The portion of the heap available to the running application program and the Toolbox.

application heap limit: The boundary between the space available for the application heap and the space available for the stack.

application heap zone: The heap zone initially provided by the Memory Manager for use by the application program and the Toolbox; initially equivalent to the application heap, but may be subdivided into two or more independent heap zones.

application list: A data structure, kept in the Desktop file, for launching applications from their documents in the hierarchical file system. For each application in the list, an entry is maintained that includes the name and signature of the application, as well as the directory ID of the folder containing it.

application parameters: Thirty-two bytes of memory, located above the application globals, reserved for system use. The first application parameter is the address of the first QuickDraw global variable.

application space: Memory that's available for dynamic allocation by applications.

application window: A window created as the result of something done by the application, either directly or indirectly (as through the Dialog Manager).

arbitration phase: The phase in which an initiator attempts to gain control of the bus.

ascent: The vertical distance from a font's base line to its ascent line.

ascent line: A horizontal line that coincides with the tops of the tallest characters in a font.

asynchronous communication: A method of data transmission where the receiving and sending devices don't share a common timer, and no timing data is transmitted.

asynchronous execution: After calling a routine asynchronously, an application is free to perform other tasks until the routine is completed.

at-least-once transaction: An ATP transaction in which the requested operation is performed at least once, and possibly several times.

ATP: See **AppleTalk Transaction Protocol**.

auto-key event: An event generated repeatedly when the user presses and holds down a character key on the keyboard or keypad.

auto-key rate: The rate at which a character key repeats after it's begun to do so.

auto-key threshold: The length of time a character key must be held down before it begins to repeat.

auxiliary control record: A Control Manager data structure containing the information needed for drawing controls in color.

auxiliary window record: A Window Manager data structure that stores the color information needed for each color window.

background activity: A program or process that runs while the user is engaged with another application.

background procedure: A procedure passed to the Printing Manager to be run during idle times in the printing process.

base line: A horizontal line that coincides with the bottom of each character in a font, excluding descenders (such as the tail of a "p").

baud rate: The measure of the total number of bits sent over a transmission line per second.

Binary-Decimal Conversion Package: A Macintosh package for converting integers to decimal strings and vice versa.

bit image: A collection of bits in memory that have a rectilinear representation. The screen is a visible bit image.

bit map: A set of bits that represent the position and state of a corresponding set of items; in QuickDraw, a pointer to a bit image, the row width of that image, and its boundary rectangle.

BIU (bus interface unit): For the Macintosh II: The electronics connecting the MC68020 bus to the NuBus.

block: A group regarded as a unit; usually refers to data or memory in which data is stored. See **allocation block** and **memory block**.

block contents: The area that's available for use in a memory block.

block device: A device that reads and writes blocks of bytes at a time. It can read or write any accessible block on demand.

block header: The internal "housekeeping" information maintained by the Memory Manager at the beginning of each block in a heap zone.

block map: Same as **volume allocation block map.**

board sResource list: A standard Apple sResource list that must be present in every NuBus slot card that communicates with the Paris.

boundary rectangle: A rectangle, defined as part of a QuickDraw bit map, that encloses the active area of the bit image and imposes a coordinate system on it. Its top left corner is always aligned around the first bit in the bit image.

break table: A list of templates that determine the general rules for making word divisions in a particular script.

break: The condition resulting when a device maintains its transmission line in the space state for at least one frame.

bridge: An intelligent link between two or more AppleTalk networks.

broadcast service: An ALAP service in which a frame is sent to all nodes on an AppleTalk network.

bundle: A resource that maps local IDs of resources to their actual resource IDs; used to provide mappings for file references and icon lists needed by the Finder.

bus free phase: The phase in which no SCSI device is actively using the bus.

button: A standard Macintosh control that causes some immediate or continuous action when clicked or pressed with the mouse. See also **radio button.**

byte lane: Any of the four bytes that make up the NuBus data width. NuBus slot cards may use any or all of the byte lanes to communicate with each other or with the Paris.

byte swapping: The process by which the order of bytes in each 4-byte NuBus word is changed to conform to the byte order of certain processors.

card-generic driver: A driver that is designed to work with a variety of plug-in cards.

card-specific driver: A driver that is designed to work with a single model of plug-in card.

caret-blink time: The interval between blinks of the caret that marks an insertion point.

caret: A generic term meaning a symbol that indicates where something should be inserted in text. The specific symbol used is a vertical bar (|).

catalog tree file: A file that maintains the relationships between the files and directories on a hierarchical directory volume. It corresponds to the file directory on a flat directory volume.

cdev: A resource file containing device information, used by the Control Panel.

cell: The basic component of a list from a structural point of view; a cell is a box in which a list element is displayed.

cGrafPort: The drawing environment in Color QuickDraw, including elements such as a pixel map, pixel patterns, transfer modes, and arithmetic drawing modes.

channel: A queue that's used by an application to send commands to the Sound Manager.

character code: An integer representing the character that a key or combination of keys on the keyboard or keypad stands for.

character device: A device that reads or writes a stream of characters, one at a time. It can neither skip characters nor go back to a previous character.

character image: An arrangement of bits that defines a character in a font.

character key: A key that generates a keyboard event when pressed; any key except Shift, Caps Lock, Command, or Option.

character offset: The horizontal separation between a character rectangle and a font rectangle.

character origin: The point on a base line used as a reference location for drawing a character.

character position: An index into an array containing text, starting at 0 for the first character.

character rectangle: A rectangle enclosing an entire character image. Its sides are defined by the image width and the font height.

character style: A set of stylistic variations, such as bold, italic, and underline. The empty set indicates plain text (no stylistic variations).

character width: The distance to move the pen from one character's origin to the next character's origin.

check box: A standard Macintosh control that displays a setting, either checked (on) or unchecked (off). Clicking inside a check box reverses its setting.

Chooser: A desk accessory that provides a standard interface for device drivers to solicit and accept specific choices from the user.

chunky: A pixel image in which all of a pixel's bits are stored consecutively in memory, all of a row's pixels are stored consecutively, and rowBytes indicates the offset from one row to the next.

clipping: Limiting drawing to within the bounds of a particular area.

clipping region: Same as clipRgn.

clipRgn: The region to which an application limits drawing in a grafPort.

clock chip: A special chip in which are stored parameter RAM and the current setting for the date and time. This chip is powered by a battery when the system is off, thus preserving the information.

close routine: The part of a device driver's code that implements Device Manager Close calls.

closed driver: A device driver that cannot be read from or written to.

closed file: A file without an access path. Closed files cannot be read from or written to.

clump: A group of contiguous allocation blocks. Space is allocated to a new file in clumps to promote file contiguity and avoid fragmentation.

clump size: The number of allocation blocks to be allocated to a new file.

Color Look-Up Table (CLUT): A data structure that maps color indices, specified using QuickDraw, into actual color values. Color Look-Up Tables are internal to certain types of video cards.

Color Look-Up Table device: This kind of video device contains hardware that converts an arbitrary pixel value stored in the frame buffer to some actual RGB video value, which is changeable.

Color Manager: The part of the Toolbox that supplies color-selection support for Color QuickDraw on the Macintosh II.

Color QuickDraw: The part of the Toolbox that performs color graphics operations on the Macintosh II.

color table animation: Color table animation involves changing the index entries in the video device's color table to achieve a change in color, as opposed to changing the pixel values themselves. All pixel values corresponding to the altered index entries suddenly appear on the display device in the new color.

color table: A set of colors is grouped into a QuickDraw data structure called a color table. Applications can pass a handle to this color table in order to use color entries.

command phase: The phase in which the SCSI initiator tells the target what operation to perform.

compaction: The process of moving allocated blocks within a heap zone in order to collect the free space into a single block.

complement: The numerical amount that must be added to a number to give the least number containing one more digit.

completion routine: Any application-defined code to be executed when an asynchronous call to a routine is completed.

content region: The area of a window that the application draws in.

control: An object in a window on the Macintosh screen with which the user, using the mouse, can cause instant action with visible results or change settings to modify a future action.

Control Manager: The part of the Toolbox that provides routines for creating and manipulating controls (such as buttons, check boxes, and scroll bars).

control definition function: A function called by the Control Manager when it needs to perform type-dependent operations on a particular type of control, such as drawing the control.

control definition ID: A number passed to control-creation routines to indicate the type of control. It consists of the control definition function's resource ID and a variation code.

control information: Information transmitted by an application to a device driver. It may select modes of operation, start or stop processes, enable buffers, choose protocols, and so on.

control list: A list of all the controls associated with a given window.

control record: The internal representation of a control, where the Control Manager stores all the information it needs for its operations on that control.

control routine: The part of a device driver's code that implements Device Manager Control and KillIO calls.

control template: A resource that contains information from which the Control Manager can create a control.

coordinate plane: A two-dimensional grid. In QuickDraw, the grid coordinates are integers ranging from –32767 to 32767, and all grid lines are infinitely thin.

current heap zone: The heap zone currently under attention, to which most Memory Manager operations implicitly apply.

current resource file: The last resource file opened, unless you specify otherwise with a Resource Manager routine.

cursor: A 16-by-16 bit image that appears on the screen and is controlled by the mouse; called the "pointer" in Macintosh user manuals.

cursor level: A value, initialized by InitCursor, that keeps track of the number of times the cursor has been hidden.

data bits: Data communications bits that encode transmitted characters.

data buffer: Heap space containing information to be written to a file or device driver from an application, or read from a file or device driver to an application.

data fork: The part of a file that contains data accessed via the File Manager.

data mark: In a sector, information that primarily contains data from an application.

data phase: The phase in which the actual transfer of data between an SCSI initiator and target takes place.

Datagram Delivery Protocol (DDP): An AppleTalk protocol that's an ALAP client, managing socket-to-socket delivery of datagrams over AppleTalk internets.

datagram: A packet of data transmitted by DDP.

date/time record: An alternate representation of the date and time (which is stored on the clock chip in seconds since midnight, January 1, 1904).

DDP: See **Datagram Delivery Protocol**

declaration ROM: A ROM on a NuBus slot card that contains information about the card and may also contain code or other data.

default button: In an alert box or modal dialog, the button whose effect will occur if the user presses Return or Enter. In an alert box, it's boldly outlined; in a modal dialog, it's boldly outlined or the OK button.

default directory: A directory that will be used in File Manager routines whenever no other directory is specified. It may be the root directory, in which case the default directory is equivalent to the default volume.

default volume: A volume that will receive I/O during a File Manager routine call, whenever no other volume is specified.

deny modes: File access modes that include both the access rights of that path and denial of access to others.

dereference: To refer to a block by its master pointer instead of its handle.

descent: The vertical distance from a font's base line to its descent line.

descent line: A horizontal line that coincides with the bottoms of the characters in a font that extend furthest below the base line.

Desk Manager: The part of the Toolbox that supports the use of desk accessories from an application.

desk accessory: A "mini-application", implemented as a device driver, that can be run at the same time as a Macintosh application.

desk scrap: The place where data is stored when it's cut (or copied) and pasted among applications and desk accessories.

desktop: The screen as a surface for doing work on the Macintosh.

Desktop file: A resource file in which the Finder stores the version data, bundle, icons, and file references for each application on the volume.

destination rectangle: In TextEdit, the rectangle in which the text is drawn.

device: A part of the Macintosh, or a piece of external equipment, that can transfer information into or out of the Macintosh.

device address: A value in the range $00–$0F assigned to each device connected to the Apple DeskTop Bus.

device control entry: A 40-byte relocatable block of heap space that tells the Device Manager the location of a driver's routines, the location of a driver's I/O queue, and other information.

device driver event: An event generated by one of the Macintosh's device drivers.

device driver: A program that controls the exchange of information between an application and a device.

device handler ID: A value that identifies the kind of device connected to the Apple DeskTop Bus.

DeviceList: A linked list containing the gDevice records for a system. One handle to a gDevice record is allocated and initialized for each video card found by the system.

Device Manager: The part of the Operating System that supports device I/O.

device partition map: A data structure that must be placed at the start of physical block 1 of an SCSI device to enable it to perform Macintosh system startup. It describes the allocation of blocks on the device.

device resource file: An extension of the printer resource file, this file contains all the resources needed by the Chooser for operating a particular device (including the device driver code).

dial: A control with a moving indicator that displays a quantitative setting or value. Depending on the type of dial, the user may be able to change the setting by dragging the indicator with the mouse.

dialog: Same as **dialog box**.

dialog box: A box that a Macintosh application displays to request information it needs to complete a command, or to report that it's waiting for a process to complete.

Dialog Manager: The part of the Toolbox that provides routines for implementing dialogs and alerts.

dialog record: The internal representation of a dialog, where the Dialog Manager stores all the information it needs for its operations on that dialog.

dialog template: A resource that contains information from which the Dialog Manager can create a dialog.

dialog window: The window in which a dialog box is displayed.

dimmed: Drawn in gray rather than black

direct device: A video device that has a direct correlation between the value placed in the video card and the color you see on the screen.

directory ID: A unique number assigned to a directory, which the File Manager uses to distinguish it from other directories on the volume. (It's functionally equivalent to the file number assigned to a file; in fact, both directory IDs and file numbers are assigned from the same set of numbers.)

directory: A subdivision of a volume that can contain files as well as other directories; equivalent to a folder.

disabled: A disabled menu item or menu is one that cannot be chosen; the menu item or menu title appears dimmed. A disabled item in a dialog or alert box has no effect when clicked.

Disk Driver: The device driver that controls data storage and retrieval on 3 1/2-inch disks.

Disk Initialization Package: A Macintosh package for initializing and naming new disks; called by the Standard File Package.

disk-inserted event: An event generated when the user inserts a disk in a disk drive or takes any other action that requires a volume to be mounted.

display rectangle: A rectangle that determines where an item is displayed within a dialog or alert box.

dithering: A technique for mixing existing colors together to create the illusion of a third color that may be unavailable on a particular device.

document window: The standard Macintosh window for presenting a document.

double-click time: The greatest interval between a mouse-up and mouse-down event that would qualify two mouse clicks as a double-click.

draft printing: Printing a document immediately as it's drawn in the printing grafPort.

drag delay: A length of time that allows a user to drag diagonally across a main menu, moving from a submenu title into the submenu itself without the submenu disappearing.

drag region: A region in a window frame. Dragging inside this region moves the window to a new location and makes it the active window unless the Command key was down.

drive number: A number used to identify a disk drive. The internal drive is number 1, the external drive is number 2, and any additional drives will have larger numbers.

drive queue: A list of disk drives connected to the Macintosh.

drive queue: A list of disk drives connected to the Macintosh.

driver descriptor map: A data structure that must be placed at the start of physical block 0 of an SCSI device to enable it to perform Macintosh system startup. It identifies the various device drivers on the device.

driver I/O queue: A queue containing the parameter blocks of all I/O requests for one device driver.

driver name: A sequence of up to 255 printing characters used to refer to an open device driver. Driver names always begin with a period (.).

driver reference number: A number from −1 to −32 that uniquely identifies an individual device driver.

Echo Protocol: An echoing service provided on static socket number 4 (the echoer socket) by which any correctly-formed packet will be echoed back to its sender.

edit record: A complete editing environment in TextEdit, which includes the text to be edited, the grafPort and rectangle in which to display the text, the arrangement of the text within the rectangle, and other editing and display information.

empty handle: A handle that points to a NIL master pointer, signifying that the underlying relocatable block has been purged.

empty shape: A shape that contains no bits, such as one defined by only a single point.

end-of-file: See **logical end-of-file** or **physical end-of-file**.

entity name: An identifier for an entity, of the form object:type@zone.

event: A notification to an application of some occurrence that the application may want to respond to.

event code: An integer representing a particular type of event.

Event Manager: See **Toolbox Event Manager** or **Operating System Event Manager**.

event mask: A parameter passed to an Event Manager routine to specify which types of events the routine should apply to.

event message: A field of an event record containing information specific to the particular type of event.

event queue: The Operating System Event Manager's list of pending events.

event record: The internal representation of an event, through which your program learns all pertinent information about that event.

exactly-once transaction: An ATP transaction in which the requested operation is performed only once.

exception: An error or abnormal condition detected by the processor in the course of program execution; includes interrupts and traps.

exception vector: One of 64 vectors in low memory that point to the routines that are to get control in the event of an exception.

extent: A series of contiguous allocation blocks.

extent descriptor: A description of an extent, consisting of the number of the first allocation block of the extent followed by the length of the extent in blocks.

extent record: A data record, stored in the leaf nodes of the extents tree file, that contains three extent descriptors and a key identifying the record.

extents tree file: A file that contains the locations of the files on a volume.

external reference: A reference to a routine or variable defined in a separate compilation or assembly.

family record: A data structure, derived from a family resource, that contains all the information describing a font family.

file: A named, ordered sequence of bytes; a principal means by which data is stored and transmitted on the Macintosh.

file catalog: A hierarchical file directory.

file control block: A fixed-length data structure, contained in the file-control-block buffer, where information about an access path is stored.

file directory: The part of a volume that contains descriptions and locations of all the files and directories on the volume. There are two types of file directories: hierarchical file directories and flat file directories.

file I/O queue: A queue containing parameter blocks for all I/O requests to the File Manager.

File Manager: The part of the Operating System that supports file I/O.

file name: A sequence of up to 255 printing characters, excluding colons (:), that identifies a file.

file number: A unique number assigned to a file, which the File Manager uses to distinguish it from other files on the volume. A file number specifies the file's entry in a file directory.

file reference: A resource that provides the Finder with file and icon information about an application.

file tags: Information associated with each logical block, designed to allow reconstruction of files on a volume whose directory or other file-access information has been destroyed.

file tags buffer: A location in memory where file tags are read from and written to.

file type: A four-character sequence, specified when a file is created, that identifies the type of file.

file-control-block buffer: A nonrelocatable block in the system heap that contains one file control block for each access path.

Finder information: Information that the Finder provides to an application upon starting it up, telling it which documents to open or print.

fixed device: A video device that converts a pixel value to some actual RGB video value, but the hardware colors can't be changed.

fixed-point number: A signed 32-bit quantity containing an integer part in the high-order word and a fractional part in the low-order word.

fixed-width font: A font whose characters all have the same width.

Floating-Point Arithmetic Package: A Macintosh package that supports extended-precision arithmetic according to IEEE Standard 754.

font: A complete set of characters of one typeface, which may be restricted to a particular size and style, or may comprise multiple sizes, or multiple sizes and styles, as in the context of menus.

font characterization table: A table of parameters in a device driver that specifies how best to adapt fonts to that device.

font family: A group of fonts of one basic design but with variations like weight and slant.

font height: The vertical distance from a font's ascent line to its descent line.

Font Manager: The part of the Toolbox that supports the use of various character fonts for QuickDraw when it draws text.

font number: The number by which you identify a font to QuickDraw or the Font Manager.

font record: A data structure, derived from a font resource, that contains all the information describing a font.

font rectangle: The smallest rectangle enclosing all the character images in a font, if the images were all superimposed over the same character origin.

font script: The script used by the font currently designated by thePort; hence the system that determines in what form text characters are displayed to the user.

font size: The size of a font in points; equivalent to the distance between the ascent line of one line of text and the ascent line of the next line of single-spaced text.

fork: One of the two parts of a file; see **data fork** and **resource fork.**

format block: A structure in a declaration ROM that provides a standard entry point for other structures in the ROM.

four-tone record: A data structure describing the tones produced by a four-tone synthesizer.

four-tone synthesizer: The part of the Sound Driver used to make simple harmonic tones, with up to four "voices" producing sound simultaneously.

frame: The time elapsed from the start bit to the last stop bit during serial communication.

frame buffer: A buffer memory in which is stored all the picture elements (pixels) of a frame of video information.

Frame Buffer Controller (FBC): A register-controlled CMOS gate array used to generate and control video data and timing signals.

frame check sequence: A 16-bit value generated by the AppleTalk hardware, used by the receiving node to detect transmission errors.

frame header: Information at the beginning of a packet.

frame pointer: A pointer to the end of the local variables within a routine's stack frame, held in an address register and manipulated with the LINK and UNLK instructions.

frame trailer: Information at the end of an ALAP frame.

framed shape: A shape that's drawn outlined and hollow.

framing error: The condition resulting when a device doesn't receive a stop bit when expected.

free block: A memory block containing space available for allocation.

free-form synthesizer: The part of the Sound Driver used to make complex music and speech.

frequency: The number of cycles per second (also called hertz) at which a wave oscillates.

full pathname: A pathname beginning from the root directory.

full-duplex communication: A method of data transmission where two devices transmit data simultaneously.

gamma table: A table that compensates for nonlinearities in a monitor's color response.

gDevice: A QuickDraw data structure that allows an application to access a given device. A gDevice is a logical device, which the software treats the same whether it is a video card, a display device, or an offscreen pixel map.

global coordinate system: The coordinate system based on the top left corner of the bit image being at (0,0).

global width table: A data structure in the system heap used by the Font Manager to communicate fractional character widths to QuickDraw.

go-away region: A region in a window frame. Clicking inside this region of the active window makes the window close or disappear.

grafPort: A complete drawing environment, including such elements as a bit map, a subset of it in which to draw, a character font, patterns for drawing and erasing, and other pen characteristics.

graphics device: A video card, a printer, a display device, or an offscreen pixel map. Any of these device types may be used with Color QuickDraw.

GrayRgn: The global variable that in the multiple screen desktop describes and defines the desktop, the area on which windows can be dragged.

grow image: The image pulled around when the user drags inside the grow region; whatever is appropriate to show that the window's size will change.

grow region: A window region, usually within the content region, where dragging changes the size of an active window.

grow zone function: A function supplied by the application program to help the Memory Manager create free space within a heap zone.

handle: A pointer to a master pointer, which designates a relocatable block in the heap by double indirection.

hardware overrun error: The condition that occurs when the SCC's buffer becomes full.

heap: The area of memory in which space is dynamically allocated and released on demand, using the Memory Manager.

heap zone: An area of memory initialized by the Memory Manager for heap allocation.

hierarchical menu: A menu that includes, among its various menu choices, the ability to display a submenu. In most cases the submenu appears to the right of the menu item used to select it, and is marked with a filled triangle indicator.

highlight: To display an object on the screen in a distinctive visual way, such as inverting it.

horizontal blanking interval: The time between the display of the rightmost pixel on one line and the leftmost pixel on the next line.

hotSpot: The point in a cursor that's aligned with the mouse location.

I/O queue: See **driver I/O queue** or **file I/O queue**.

I/O request: A request for input from or output to a file or device driver; caused by calling a File Manager or Device Manager routine asynchronously.

icon: A 32-by-32 bit image that graphically represents an object, concept, or message.

icon list: A resource consisting of a list of icons.

icon number: A digit from 1 to 255 to which the Menu Manager adds 256 to get the resource ID of an icon associated with a menu item.

image width: The width of a character image.

inactive control: A control that won't respond to the user's actions with the mouse. An inactive control is highlighted in some special way, such as dimmed.

inactive window: Any window that isn't the frontmost window on the desktop.

indicator: The moving part of a dial that displays its current setting.

initiator device: An SCSI device that initiates a communication by asking another device (known as the target device) to perform a certain operation.

input driver: A device driver that receives serial data via a serial port and transfers it to an application.

insertion point: An empty selection range; the character position where text will be inserted (usually marked with a blinking caret).

interface routine: A routine called from Pascal whose purpose is to trap to a certain Toolbox or Operating System routine.

International Utilities Package: A Macintosh package that gives you access to country-dependent information such as the formats for numbers, currency, dates, and times.

internet: An interconnected group of AppleTalk networks.

internet address: The AppleTalk address and network number of a socket.

interrupt: An exception that's signaled to the processor by a device, to notify the processor of a change in condition of the device, such as the completion of an I/O request.

interrupt handler: A routine that services interrupts.

interrupt priority level: A number identifying the importance of the interrupt. It indicates which device is interrupting, and which interrupt handler should be executed.

interrupt vector: A pointer to an interrupt handler.

invalidation: When a color table is modified, its inverse table must be rebuilt, and the screen should be redrawn to take advantage of this new information. Rather than being reconstructed when the color table is changed, the inverse table is marked invalid, and is automatically rebuilt when next accessed.

inverse table: A special Color Manager data structure arranged in such a manner that, given an arbitrary RGB color, the pixel value can be very rapidly looked up.

invert: To highlight by changing white pixels to black and vice versa.

invisible control: A control that's not drawn in its window.

invisible window: A window that's not drawn in its plane on the desktop.

item: In dialog and alert boxes, a control, icon, picture, or piece of text, each displayed inside its own display rectangle. See also **menu item**.

item list: A list of information about all the items in a dialog or alert box.

item number: The index, starting from 1, of an item in an item list.

IWM: "Integrated Woz Machine"; the custom chip that controls the 3 1/2-inch disk drives.

job dialog: A dialog that sets information about one printing job; associated with the Print command.

journal code: A code passed by a Toolbox Event Manager routine in its Control call to the journaling device driver, to designate which routine is making the Control call.

journaling mechanism: A mechanism that allows you to feed the Toolbox Event Manager events from some source other than the user.

jump table: A table that contains one entry for every routine in an application and is the means by which the loading and unloading of segments is implemented.

justification: The horizontal placement of lines of text relative to the edges of the rectangle in which the text is drawn.

justification gap: The number of pixels that must be added to a line of text to make it exactly fill a given measure. Also called slop.

kern: To draw part of a character so that it overlaps an adjacent character.

key code: An integer representing a key on the keyboard or keypad, without reference to the character that the key stands for.

key script: The system that determines the keyboard layout and input method for the user interface. It may be different from the font script, which determines how text is displayed.

key-down event: An event generated when the user presses a character key on the keyboard or keypad.

key-up event: An event generated when the user releases a character key on the keyboard or keypad.

keyboard configuration: A resource that defines a particular keyboard layout by associating a character code with each key or combination of keys on the keyboard or keypad.

keyboard equivalent: The combination of the Command key and another key, used to invoke a menu item from the keyboard.

keyboard event: An event generated when the user presses, releases, or holds down a character key on the keyboard or keypad; any key-down, key-up, or auto-key event.

leading: The amount of blank vertical space between the descent line of one line of text and the ascent line of the next line of single-spaced text.

ligature: A character that combines two letters.

line-height table: A TextEdit data structure that holds vertical spacing information for an edit record's text.

List Manager: The part of the Operating System that provides routines for creating, displaying, and manipulating lists.

list definition procedure: A procedure called by the List Manager that determines the appearance and behavior of a list.

list element: The basic component of a list from a logical point of view, a list element is simply bytes of data. In a list of names, for instance, the name Melvin might be a list element.

list record: The internal representation of a list, where the List Manager stores all the information it requires for its operations on that list.

list separator: The character that separates numbers, as when a list of numbers is entered by the user.

local coordinate system: The coordinate system local to a grafPort, imposed by the boundary rectangle defined in its bit map.

local ID: A number that refers to an icon list or file reference in an application's resource file and is mapped to an actual resource ID by a bundle.

localization: The process of adapting an application to different languages, including converting its user interface to a different script.

location table: An array of words (one for each character in a font) that specifies the location of each character's image in the font's bit image.

lock: To temporarily prevent a relocatable block from being moved during heap compaction.

lock bit: A bit in the master pointer to a relocatable block that indicates whether the block is currently locked.

locked file: A file whose data cannot be changed.

locked volume: A volume whose data cannot be changed. Volumes can be locked by either a software flag or a mechanical setting.

logical block: Volume space composed of 512 consecutive bytes of standard information and an additional number of bytes of information specific to the Disk Driver.

logical end-of-file: The position of one byte past the last byte in a file; equal to the actual number of bytes in the file.

logical size: The number of bytes in a memory block's contents.

luminance: The intensity of light. Two colors with different luminances will be displayed at different intensities.

M.I.D.I. synthesizer: This synthesizer interfaces with external synthesizers via a Musical Instrument Data Interface (M.I.D.I.) adaptor connected to the serial ports.

magnitude: The vertical distance between any given point on a wave and the horizontal line about which the wave oscillates.

main event loop: In a standard Macintosh application program, a loop that repeatedly calls the Toolbox Event Manager to get events and then responds to them as appropriate.

main screen: On a system with multiple display devices, the screen with the menu bar is called the main screen.

main segment: The segment containing the main program.

mark state: The state of a transmission line indicating a binary 1.

mark: A marker used by the File Manager to keep track of where it is during a read or write operation. It is the position of the next byte in a file that will be read or written.

master directory block: Part of the data structure of a flat directory volume; contains the volume information and the volume allocation block map.

master pointer: A single pointer to a relocatable block, maintained by the Memory Manager and updated whenever the block is moved, purged, or reallocated. All handles to a relocatable block refer to it by double indirection through the master pointer.

Memory Manager: The part of the Operating System that dynamically allocates and releases memory space in the heap.

memory block: An area of contiguous memory within a heap zone.

menu: A list of menu items that appears when the user points to a menu title in the menu bar and presses the mouse button. Dragging through the menu and releasing over an enabled menu item chooses that item.

menu bar: The horizontal strip at the top of the Macintosh screen that contains the menu titles of all menus in the menu list.

menu definition procedure: A procedure called by the Menu Manager when it needs to perform type-dependent operations on a particular type of menu, such as drawing the menu.

menu entry: An entry in a menu color table that defines color values for the menu's title, bar, and items.

menu ID: A number in the menu record that identifies the menu.

menu item: A choice in a menu, usually a command to the current application.

menu item number: The index, starting from 1, of a menu item in a menu.

menu list: A list containing menu handles for all menus in the menu bar, along with information on the position of each menu.

Menu Manager: The part of the Toolbox that deals with setting up menus and letting the user choose from them.

menu record: The internal representation of a menu, where the Menu Manager stores all the information it needs for its operations on that menu.

menu title: A word or phrase in the menu bar that designates one menu.

message phase: The phase in which the target sends one byte of message information back to the initiator.

missing symbol: A character to be drawn in case of a request to draw a character that's missing from a particular font.

modal dialog: A dialog that requires the user to respond before doing any other work on the desktop.

modeless dialog: A dialog that allows the user to work elsewhere on the desktop before responding.

modifier: A program that interprets and processes Sound Manager commands as they pass through a channel.

modifier key: A key (Shift, Caps Lock, Option, or Command) that generates no keyboard events of its own, but changes the meaning of other keys or mouse actions.

mounted volume: A volume that previously was inserted into a disk drive and had descriptive information read from it by the File Manager.

mouse-down event: An event generated when the user presses the mouse button.

mouse scaling: A feature that causes the cursor to move twice as far during a mouse stroke than it would have otherwise, provided the change in the cursor's position exceeds the mouse-scaling threshold within one tick after the mouse is moved.

mouse-scaling threshold: A number of pixels which, if exceeded by the sum of the horizontal and vertical changes in the cursor position during one tick of mouse movement, causes mouse scaling to occur (if that feature is turned on); normally six pixels.

mouse-up event: An event generated when the user releases the mouse button.

Name-Binding Protocol (NBP): An AppleTalk protocol that's a DDP client, used to convert entity names to their internet socket addresses.

name lookup: An NBP operation that allows clients to obtain the internet addresses of entities from their names.

names directory: The union of all name tables in an internet.

names information socket: The socket in a node used to implement NBP (always socket number 2).

names table: A list of each entity's name and internet address in a node.

NBP tuple: An entity name and an internet address.

NBP: See **Name-Binding Protocol.**

network event: An event generated by the AppleTalk Manager.

network number: An identifier for an AppleTalk network.

network-visible entity: A named socket client on an internet.

newline character: Any character, but usually Return (ASCII code $0D), that indicates the end of a sequence of bytes.

newline mode: A mode of reading data where the end of the data is indicated by a newline character (and not by a specific byte count).

node ID: A number, dynamically assigned, that identifies a node.

node: A device that's attached to and communicates via an AppleTalk network.

nonbreaking space: The character with ASCII code $CA; drawn as a space the same width as a digit, but interpreted as a nonblank character for the purposes of word wraparound and selection.

nonrelocatable block: A block whose location in the heap is fixed and can't be moved during heap compaction.

note synthesizer: Functionally equivalent to the old square-wave synthesizer, the note sysntesizer lets you generate simple melodies and informative sounds such as error warnings.

null event: An event reported when there are no other events to report.

null-style record: A TextEdit data structure used to store the style information for a null selection.

off-line volume: A mounted volume with all but the volume control block released.

offset/width table: An array of words that specifies the character offsets and character widths of all characters in a font.

offspring: For a given directory, the set of files and directories for which it is the parent.

on-line volume: A mounted volume with its volume buffer and descriptive information contained in memory.

open driver: A driver that can be read from and written to.

open file: A file with an access path. Open files can be read from and written to.

open permission: Information about a file that indicates whether the file can be read from, written to, or both.

open routine: The part of a device driver's code that implements Device Manager Open calls.

Operating System: The lowest-level software in the Macintosh. It does basic tasks such as I/O, memory management, and interrupt handling.

Operating System Event Manager: The part of the Operating System that reports hardware-related events such as mouse-button presses and keystrokes.

Operating System Utilities: Operating System routines that perform miscellaneous tasks such as getting the date and time, finding out the user's preferred speaker volume and other preferences, and doing simple string comparison.

output driver: A device driver that receives data via a serial port and transfers it to an application.

overrun error: See **hardware overrun error** and **software overrun error**.

Package Manager: The part of the Toolbox that lets you access Macintosh RAM-based packages.

package: A set of routines and data types that's stored as a resource and brought into memory only when needed.

page rectangle: The rectangle marking the boundaries of a printed page image. The boundary rectangle, portRect, and clipRgn of the printing grafPort are set to this rectangle.

palette: A collection of small symbols, usually enclosed in rectangles, that represent operations that can be selected by the user. Also, a collection of colors provided and used by your application according to your needs.

Palette Manager: The part of the Toolbox that establishes and monitors the color environment of the Macintosh II. It gives preference to the color needs of the front window, making the assumption that the front window is of greatest interest to the user.

pane: An independently scrollable area of a window, for showing a different part of the same document.

panel: An area of a window that shows a different interpretation of the same part of a document.

paper rectangle: The rectangle marking the boundaries of the physical sheet of paper on which a page is printed.

parameter block: A data structure used to transfer information between applications and certain Operating System routines.

parameter RAM: In the clock chip, 20 bytes where settings such as those made with the Control Panel desk accessory are preserved.

parent: For a given file or directory, the directory immediately above it in the tree.

parent ID: The directory ID of the directory containing a file or directory.

parity bit: A data communications bit used to verify that data bits received by a device match the data bits transmitted by another device.

parity error: The condition resulting when the parity bit received by a device isn't what was expected.

part code: An integer between 1 and 253 that stands for a particular part of a control (possibly the entire control).

partial pathname: A pathname beginning from any directory other than the root directory.

path reference number: A number that uniquely identifies an individual access path; assigned when the access path is created.

pathname: A series of concatenated directory and file names that identifies a given file or directory. See also **partial pathname** and **full pathname**.

pattern: An 8-by-8 bit image, used to define a repeating design (such as stripes) or tone (such as gray).

pattern transfer mode: One of eight transfer modes for drawing lines or shapes with a pattern.

period: The time elapsed during one complete cycle of a wave.

phase: Some fraction of a wave cycle (measured from a fixed point on the wave).

physical end-of-file: The position of one byte past the last allocation block of a file; equal to 1 more than the maximum number of bytes the file can contain.

physical size: The actual number of bytes a memory block occupies within its heap zone.

picture: A saved sequence of QuickDraw drawing commands (and, optionally, picture comments) that you can play back later with a single procedure call; also, the image resulting from these commands.

picture comments: Data stored in the definition of a picture that doesn't affect the picture's appearance but may be used to provide additional information about the picture when it's played back.

picture frame: A rectangle, defined as part of a picture, that surrounds the picture and gives a frame of reference for scaling when the picture is played back.

PIO (programmed input/output): An interfacing technique where the processor directly accesses registers assigned to I/O devices by executing processor instructions. Memory mapped I/O port registers are addressed as memory locations.

pixel: A dot on a display screen. Pixel is short for picture element.

pixel map: Color QuickDraw's extended data structure, containing the dimensions and content of a pixel image, plus information on the image's storage format, depth, resolution, and color usage.

pixel pattern: The pattern structure used by Color QuickDraw, one of three types: old-style pattern, full color pixel pattern, or RGB pattern.

pixel value: The bits in a pixel, taken together, form a number known as the pixel value. Color QuickDraw represents each pixel on the screen using one, two, four, or eight bits in memory.

plane: The front-to-back position of a window on the desktop.

point: The intersection of a horizontal grid line and a vertical grid line on the coordinate plane, defined by a horizontal and a vertical coordinate; also, a typographical term meaning approximately 1/72 inch.

polygon: A sequence of connected lines, defined by QuickDraw line-drawing commands.

pop-up menu: A menu not located in the menu bar, which appears when the user presses the mouse button in a particular place.

port: See **grafPort**.

portBits: The bit map of a grafPort.

portRect: A rectangle, defined as part of a grafPort, that encloses a subset of the bit map for use by the grafPort.

post: To place an event in the event queue for later processing.

prime routine: The part of a device driver's code that implements Device Manager Read and Write calls.

print record: A record containing all the information needed by the Printing Manager to perform a particular printing job.

Printer Driver: The device driver for the currently installed printer.

printer resource file: A file containing all the resources needed to run the Printing Manager with a particular printer.

Printing Manager: The routines and data types that enable applications to communicate with the Printer Driver to print on any variety of printer via the same interface.

printing grafPort: A special grafPort customized for printing instead of drawing on the screen.

processor priority: Bits 8-10 of the MC68000's status register, indicating which interrupts will be processed and which will be ignored.

proportional font: A font whose characters all have character widths that are proportional to their image width.

protocol: A well-defined set of communications rules.

protocol handler table: A list of the protocol handlers for a node.

protocol handler: A software process in a node that recognizes different kinds of frames by their ALAP type and services them.

purge: To remove a relocatable block from the heap, leaving its master pointer allocated but set to NIL.

purge bit: A bit in the master pointer to a relocatable block that indicates whether the block is currently purgeable.

purge warning procedure: A procedure associated with a particular heap zone that's called whenever a block is purged from that zone.

purgeable block: A relocatable block that can be purged from the heap.

queue: A list of identically structured entries linked together by pointers.

QuickDraw: The part of the Toolbox that performs all graphic operations on the Macintosh screen.

radio button: A standard Macintosh control that displays a setting, either on or off, and is part of a group in which only one button can be on at a time.

RAM: The Macintosh's random access memory, which contains exception vectors, buffers used by hardware devices, the system and application heaps, the stack, and other information used by applications.

range locking: Locking a range of bytes in a file so that other users can't read from or write to that range, but allowing the rest of the file to be accessed.

raw key codes: Hardware-produced key codes on the Macintosh II and Apple Extended Keyboard, which are translated into **virtual key codes** by the 'KMAP' resource.

read/write permission: Information associated with an access path that indicates whether the file can be read from, written to, both read from and written to, or whatever the file's open permission allows.

reallocate: To allocate new space in the heap for a purged block, updating its master pointer to point to its new location.

reference number: A number greater than 0, returned by the Resource Manager when a resource file is opened, by which you can refer to that file. In Resource Manager routines that expect a reference number, 0 represents the system resource file.

reference value: In a window record or control record, a 32-bit field that an application program may store into and access for any purpose.

region: An arbitrary area or set of areas on the QuickDraw coordinate plane. The outline of a region should be one or more closed loops.

register-based routine: A Toolbox or Operating System routine that receives its parameters and returns its results, if any, in registers.

relative handle: A handle to a relocatable block expressed as the offset of its master pointer within the heap zone, rather than as the absolute memory address of the master pointer.

release: To free an allocated area of memory, making it available for reuse.

release timer: A timer for determining when an exactly-once response buffer can be released.

relocatable block: A block that can be moved within the heap during compaction.

reselection phase: An optional phase in which the SCSI initiator allows a target device to reconnect itself to the initiator.

resource: Data or code stored in a resource file and managed by the Resource Manager.

resource attribute: One of several characteristics, specified by bits in a resource reference, that determine how the resource should be dealt with.

resource data: In a resource file, the data that comprises a resource.

resource file: The resource fork of a file.

resource fork: The part of a file that contains data used by an application (such as menus, fonts, and icons). The resource fork of an application file also contains the application code itself.

resource header: At the beginning of a resource file, data that gives the offsets to and lengths of the resource data and resource map.

resource ID: A number that, together with the resource type, identifies a resource in a resource file. Every resource has an ID number.

Resource Manager: The part of the Toolbox that reads and writes resources.

resource map: In a resource file, data that is read into memory when the file is opened and that, given a resource specification, leads to the corresponding resource data.

resource name: A string that, together with the resource type, identifies a resource in a resource file. A resource may or may not have a name.

resource reference: In a resource map, an entry that identifies a resource and contains either an offset to its resource data in the resource file or a handle to the data if it's already been read into memory.

resource specification: A resource type and either a resource ID or a resource name.

resource type: The type of a resource in a resource file, designated by a sequence of four characters (such as 'MENU' for a menu).

response BDS: A data structure used to pass response information to the ATP module.

result code: An integer indicating whether a routine completed its task successfully or was prevented by some error condition (or other special condition, such as reaching the end of a file).

resume procedure: A procedure within an application that allows the application to recover from system errors.

retry count: The maximum number of retransmissions for an NBP or ATP packet.

retry interval: The time between retransmissions of a packet by NBP or ATP.

RGB space: How Color QuickDraw represents colors. Each color has a red, a green, and a blue component, hence the name RGB.

RGB value: Color QuickDraw represents color using the RGBColor record type, which specifies the red, green, and blue components of the color. The RGBColor record is used by an application specifies the colors it needs. The translation from the RGB value to the pixel value is performed at the time the color is drawn.

ROM: The Macintosh's permanent read-only memory, which contains the routines for the Toolbox and Operating System, and the various system traps.

root directory: The directory at the base of a file catalog.

routine selector: A value pushed on the stack to select a particular routine from a group of routines called by a single trap macro.

Routing Table Maintenance Protocol (RTMP): An AppleTalk protocol that's used internally by AppleTalk to maintain tables for routing datagrams through an internet.

routing table: A table in a bridge that contains routing information.

row width: The number of bytes in each row of a bit image.

RTMP: See **Routing Table Maintenance Protocol**.

RTMP socket: The socket in a node used to implement RTMP.

RTMP stub: The RTMP code in a nonbridge node.

sampled sound synthesizer: Functionally equivalent to the old free-form synthesizer, the sample sound synthesizer lets you play pre-recorded sounds or sounds generated by your application.

scaling factor: A value, given as a fraction, that specifies the amount a character should be stretched or shrunk before it's drawn.

SCC: See **Serial Communications Controller**.

Scrap Manager: The part of the Toolbox that enables cutting and pasting between applications, desk accessories, or an application and a desk accessory.

scrap: A place where cut or copied data is stored.

scrap file: The file containing the desk scrap (usually named "Clipboard File").

screen buffer: A block of memory from which the video display reads the information to be displayed.

script: A writing system, such as Cyrillic or Arabic. This book is printed in Roman script.

script interface system: Special software that supports the display and manipulation of a particular script.

SCSI: See **Small Computer Standard Interface**.

SCSI Manager: The part of the Operating System that controls the exchange of information between a Macintosh and peripheral devices connected through the Small Computer Standard Interface (SCSI).

sector: Disk space composed of 512 consecutive bytes of standard information and 12 bytes of file tags.

segment: One of several parts into which the code of an application may be divided. Not all segments need to be in memory at the same time.

Segment Loader: The part of the Operating System that loads the code of an application into memory, either as a single unit or divided into dynamically loaded segments.

selection phase: The phase in which the initiator selects the target device that will be asked to perform a certain operation.

selection range: The series of characters (inversely highlighted), or the character position (marked with a blinking caret), at which the next editing operation will occur.

sequence number: A number from 0 to 7, assigned to an ATP response datagram to indicate its ordering within the response.

Serial Communications Controller (SCC): The chip that handles serial I/O through the modem and printer ports.

Serial Driver: A device driver that controls communication, via serial ports, between applications and serial peripheral devices.

serial data: Data communicated over a single-path communication line, one bit at a time.

server: A node that manages access to a peripheral device.

service request enable: A bit set by a device connected to the Apple DeskTop Bus to tell the system that it needs servicing.

session: A session consists of a series of transactions between two sockets, characterized by the orderly sequencing of requests and responses.

signature: A four-character sequence that uniquely identifies an application to the Finder.

slop: See **justification gap.**

slot exec parameter block: A data structure that provides communication with the Slot Manager routines sMacBoot and sPrimaryInit.

Slot Manager: A set of Macintosh II ROM routines that let applications access declaration ROMs on slot cards.

slot parameter block: A data structure that provides communication with all Slot Manager routines except sMacBoot and sPrimaryInit.

slot resource: A software structure in the declaration ROM of a slot card.

slot space: The upper one sixteenth of the total address space. These addresses are in the form $Fsxx xxxx where F, s, and x are hex digits of 4 bits each. This address space is geographically divided among the NuBus slots according to slot ID number.

Small Computer Standard Interface (SCSI): A specification of mechanical, electrical, and functional standards for connecting small computers with intelligent peripherals such as hard disks, printers, and optical disks.

socket: A logical entity within the node of a network.

socket client: A software process in a node that owns a socket.

socket listener: The portion of a socket client that receives and services datagrams addressed to that socket.

socket number: An identifier for a socket.

socket table: A listing of all the socket listeners for each active socket in a node.

software overrun error: The condition that occurs when an input driver's buffer becomes full.

solid shape: A shape that's filled in with any pattern.

Sound Driver: The device driver that controls sound generation in an application.

sound buffer: A block of memory from which the sound generator reads the information to create an audio waveform.

sound procedure: A procedure associated with an alert that will emit one of up to four sounds from the Macintosh's speaker. Its integer parameter ranges from 0 to 3 and specifies which sound.

source transfer mode: One of eight transfer modes for drawing text or transferring any bit image between two bit maps.

space state: The state of a transmission line indicating a binary 0.

spool printing: Writing a representation of a document's printed image to disk or to memory, and then printing it (as opposed to immediate draft printing).

square-wave synthesizer: The part of the Sound Driver used to produce less harmonic sounds than the four-tone synthesizer, such as beeps.

sResource: See **slot resource.**

sResource directory: The structure in a declaration ROM that provides access to its sResource lists.

sResource list: A list of offsets to sResources.

stack: The area of memory in which space is allocated and released in LIFO (last-in-first-out) order.

stack frame: The area of the stack used by a routine for its parameters, return address, local variables, and temporary storage.

stack-based routine: A Toolbox or Operating System routine that receives its parameters and returns its results, if any, on the stack.

stage: Every alert has four stages, corresponding to consecutive occurrences of the alert, and a different response may be specified for each stage.

Standard File Package: A Macintosh package for presenting the standard user interface when a file is to be saved or opened.

start bit: A serial data communications bit that signals that the next bits transmitted are data bits.

startup screen: When the system is started up, one of the display devices is selected as the startup screen, the screen on which the "happy Macintosh" icon appears.

status information: Information transmitted to an application by a device driver. It may indicate the current mode of operation, the readiness of the device, the occurrence of errors, and so on.

status phase: The phase in which the SCSI target sends one byte of status information back to the initiator.

status routine: The part of a device driver's code that implements Device Manager Status calls.

stop bit: A serial data communications bit that signals the end of data bits.

structure region: An entire window; its complete "structure".

style: See **character style**.

style dialog: A dialog that sets options affecting the page dimensions; associated with the Page Setup command.

style record: A TextEdit data structure that specifies the styles for the edit record's text.

style scrap: A new TextEdit scrap type, 'styl', is used for storing style information in the desk scrap along with the old 'TEXT' scrap.

style table: A TextEdit data structure that contains one entry for each distinct style used in an edit record's text.

subdirectory: Any directory other than the root directory.

submenu delay: The length of time before a submenu appears as a user drags through a hierarchical main menu; it prevents rapid flashing of submenus.

super slot space: The large portion of memory in the range $9000 0000 through $EFFF FFFF. NuBus addresses of the form $sxxx xxxx (that is, $s000 0000 through $sFFF FFFF) reference the super slot space that belongs to the card in slot s, where s is an ID digit in the range $9 through $E.

synchronous execution: After calling a routine synchronously, an application cannot continue execution until the routine is completed.

synthesizer: A program which, like a device driver, interprets Sound Manager commands and produces sound. See **free-form, four-tone,** or **square-wave synthesizer**.

synthesizer buffer: A description of the sound to be generated by a synthesizer.

System Error Handler: The part of the Operating System that assumes control when a fatal system error occurs.

system error alert table: A resource that determines the appearance and function of system error alerts.

system error alert: An alert box displayed by the System Error Handler.

system error ID: An ID number that appears in a system error alert to identify the error.

system event mask: A global event mask that controls which types of events get posted into the event queue.

system font: The font that the system uses (in menus, for example). Its name is Chicago.

system font size: The size of text drawn by the system in the system font; 12 points.

system heap: The portion of the heap reserved for use by the Operating System.

system heap zone: The heap zone provided by the Memory Manager for use by the Operating System; equivalent to the system heap.

system resource: A resource in the system resource file.

system resource file: A resource file containing standard resources, accessed if a requested resource wasn't found in any of the other resource files that were searched.

system startup information: Certain configurable system parameters that are stored in the first two logical blocks of a volume and read in at system startup.

system window: A window in which a desk accessory is displayed.

target device: An SCSI device (typically an intelligent peripheral) that receives a request from an initiator device to perform a certain operation.

text styles: TextEdit records used for communicating style information between the application program and the TextEdit routines.

TextEdit: The part of the Toolbox that supports the basic text entry and editing capabilities of a standard Macintosh application.

TextEdit scrap: The place where certain TextEdit routines store the characters most recently cut or copied from text.

theGDevice: When drawing is being performed on a device, a handle to that device is stored as a global variable **theGDevice.**

thousands separator: The character that separates every three digits to the left of the decimal point.

thumb: The Control Manager's term for the scroll box (the indicator of a scroll bar).

tick: A sixtieth of a second.

Time Manager: The part of the Operating System that lets you schedule a routine to be executed after a given number of milliseconds have elapsed.

Toolbox: Same as **User Interface Toolbox.**

Toolbox Event Manager: The part of the Toolbox that allows your application program to monitor the user's actions with the mouse, keyboard, and keypad.

Toolbox Utilities: The part of the Toolbox that performs generally useful operations such as fixed-point arithmetic, string manipulation, and logical operations on bits.

track: Disk space composed of 8 to 12 consecutive sectors. A track corresponds to one ring of constant radius around the disk.

transaction: A request-response communication between two ATP clients. See **transaction request** and **transaction response.**

transaction ID: An identifier assigned to a transaction.

transaction request: The initial part of a transaction in which one socket client asks another to perform an operation and return a response.

transaction response: The concluding part of a transaction in which one socket client returns requested information or simply confirms that a requested operation was performed.

Transcendental Functions Package: A Macintosh package that contains trigonometric, logarithmic, exponential, and financial functions, as well as a random number generator.

transfer mode: A specification of which Boolean operation QuickDraw should perform when drawing or when transferring a bit image from one bit map to another.

trap dispatch table: A table in RAM containing the addresses of all Toolbox and Operating System routines in encoded form.

trap dispatcher: The part of the Operating System that examines a trap word to determine what operation it stands for, looks up the address of the corresponding routine in the trap dispatch table, and jumps to the routine.

trap macro: A macro that assembles into a trap word, used for calling a Toolbox or Operating System routine from assembly language.

trap number: The identifying number of a Toolbox or Operating System routine; an index into the trap dispatch table.

trap word: An unimplemented instruction representing a call to a Toolbox or Operating System routine.

type coercion: Many compilers feature type coercion (also known as typecasting), which allows a data structure of one type to be converted to another type. In many cases, this conversion is simply a relaxation of type-checking in the compiler, allowing the substitution of a differently-typed but equivalent data structure.

unimplemented instruction: An instruction word that doesn't correspond to any valid machine-language instruction but instead causes a trap.

unit number: The number of each device driver's entry in the unit table.

unit table: A 128-byte nonrelocatable block containing a handle to the device control entry for each device driver.

unlock: To allow a relocatable block to be moved during heap compaction.

unmounted volume: A volume that hasn't been inserted into a disk drive and had descriptive information read from it, or a volume that previously was mounted and has since had the memory used by it released.

unpurgeable block: A relocatable block that can't be purged from the heap.

update event: An event generated by the Window Manager when a window's contents need to be redrawn.

update region: A window region consisting of all areas of the content region that have to be redrawn.

User Interface Toolbox: The software in the Macintosh ROM that helps you implement the standard Macintosh user interface in your application.

user bytes: Four bytes in an ATP header provided for use by ATP's clients.

valence: The number of offspring for a given directory.

validity status: A number stored in parameter RAM designating whether the last attempt to write there was successful. (The number is $A8 if so.)

variation code: The part of a window or control definition ID that distinguishes closely related types of windows or controls.

VBL task: A task performed during the vertical retrace interrupt.

vector table: A table of interrupt vectors in low memory.

Versatile Interface Adapter (VIA): The chip that handles most of the Macintosh's I/O and interrupts.

version data: In an application's resource file, a resource that has the application's signature as its resource type; typically a string that gives the name, version number, and date of the application.

version number: A number from 0 to 255 used to distinguish between files with the same name.

Vertical Retrace Manager: The part of the Operating System that schedules and executes tasks during the vertical retrace interrupt.

vertical blanking interrupt: See **vertical retrace interrupt**.

vertical blanking interval: The time between the display of the last pixel on the bottom line of the screen and the first one on the top line.

vertical retrace interrupt: An interrupt generated 60 times a second by the Macintosh video circuitry while the beam of the display tube returns from the bottom of the screen to the top; also known as vertical blanking interrupt.

vertical retrace queue: A list of the tasks to be executed during the vertical retrace interrupt.

VIA: See **Versatile Interface Adapter**.

view rectangle: In TextEdit, the rectangle in which the text is visible.

virtual key codes: The key codes that appear in keyboard events. (See also **raw key codes**.)

visible control: A control that's drawn in its window (but may be completely overlapped by another window or other object on the screen).

visible window: A window that's drawn in its plane on the desktop (but may be completely overlapped by another window or object on the screen).

visRgn: The region of a grafPort, manipulated by the Window Manager, that's actually visible on the screen.

volume: A piece of storage medium formatted to contain files; usually a disk or part of a disk. A 3.5-inch Macintosh disk is one volume.

volume allocation block map: A list of 12-bit entries, one for each allocation block, that indicate whether the block is currently allocated to a file, whether it's free for use, or which block is next in the file. Block maps exist both on flat directory volumes and in memory.

volume attributes: Information contained on volumes and in memory indicating whether the volume is locked, whether it's busy (in memory only), and whether the volume control block matches the volume information (in memory only).

volume bit map: A data structure containing a sequence of bits, one bit for each allocation block, that indicate whether the block is allocated or free for use. Volume bit maps exist both on hierarchical directory volumes and in memory.

volume buffer: Memory used initially to load the master directory block, and used thereafter for reading from files that are opened without an access path buffer.

volume control block: A nonrelocatable block that contains volume-specific information, including the volume information from the master directory block.

volume index: A number identifying a mounted volume listed in the volume-control-block queue. The first volume in the queue has an index of 1, and so on.

volume information block: Part of the data structure of a hierarchical directory volume; it contains the volume information.

volume information: Volume-specific information contained on a volume, including the volume name and the number of files on the volume.

volume name: A sequence of up to 27 printing characters that identifies a volume; followed by a colon (:) in File Manager routine calls, to distinguish it from a file name.

volume reference number: A unique number assigned to a volume as it's mounted, used to refer to the volume.

volume-control-block queue: A list of the volume control blocks for all mounted volumes.

wave table synthesizer: Similar to the old four-tone synthesizer, the wave table synthesizer produces complex sounds and multi-part music.

waveform description: A sequence of bytes describing a waveform.

waveform: The physical shape of a wave.

wavelength: The horizontal extent of one complete cycle of a wave.

window: An object on the desktop that presents information, such as a document or a message.

window class: In a window record, an indication of whether a window is a system window, a dialog or alert window, or a window created directly by the application.

window definition function: A function called by the Window Manager when it needs to perform certain type-dependent operations on a particular type of window, such as drawing the window frame.

window definition ID: A number passed to window-creation routines to indicate the type of window. It consists of the window definition function's resource ID and a variation code.

window frame: The structure region of a window minus its content region.

window list: A list of all windows ordered by their front-to-back positions on the desktop.

Window Manager: The part of the Toolbox that provides routines for creating and manipulating windows.

Window Manager port: A grafPort that has the entire screen as its portRect and is used by the Window Manager to draw window frames.

window record: The internal representation of a window, where the Window Manager stores all the information it needs for its operations on that window.

window template: A resource from which the Window Manager can create a window.

word wraparound: Keeping words from being split between lines when text is drawn.

word-selection break table: A **break table** that is used to find word boundaries for word selection, spelling checking, and so on.

word-wrapping break table: A **break table** that is used to find word boundaries for screen wrapping of text.

working directory: An alternative way of referring to a directory. When opened as a working directory, a directory is given a working directory reference number that's used to refer to it in File Manager calls.

working directory control block: A data structure that contains the directory ID of a working directory, as well as the volume reference number of the volume on which the directory is located.

working directory reference number: A temporary reference number used to identify a working directory. It can be used in place of the volume reference number in all File Manager calls; the File Manager uses it to get the directory ID and volume reference number from the working directory control block.

workstation: A node through which a user can access a server or other nodes.

write data structure: A data structure used to pass information to the ALAP or DDP modules.

X-Ref: An abbreviation for *cross-reference.*

zone: An arbitrary subset of AppleTalk networks in an internet. See also **heap zone.**

zone header: The internal "housekeeping" information maintained by the Memory Manager at the beginning of each heap zone.

zone pointer: A pointer to a zone record.

zone record: A data structure representing a heap zone.

zone trailer: A minimum-size free block marking the end of a heap zone.